Truth to Tell

D0620666

DAVID PAWSON

Truth to Tell

HODDER AND STOUGHTON
LONDON SYDNEY AUCKLAND TORONTO

To my grandfather, who was an evangelistic pastor;
to my father, who is a pastoral evangelist;
and to my wife, who has loyally supported a husband
endeavouring to be a little bit of both.

A Word of Explanation

THIS BOOK IS a stop-gap, in at least three ways:

First, it is an attempt to jump the gulf between *pulpit and pew*. The preacher can be a long way from his hearers, both physically and mentally. As one wise friend remarked to me when I was beginning to preach, 'It's not just getting it off your reel but on to his bobbin!' The Reformation principle that God's word must be available in a form 'understandable to the people' still stands (and is one reason why the work of Bible translation, even into English, is never finished).

Second, it attempts to bridge the gap between *exposition and experience*. Doctrine is often dull; logic can be lifeless. Experience is exciting and sensations are stimulating. There appears to me to be a gap in the publishing world between paperbacks packed with sensational experience and hardbacks solid with scholarship. But the two must be related if anything worthwhile is to happen.

Third, it seeks to meet the needs of *doubter and disciple*. These talks (and that is all they are) were given to an evening congregation in which one third were between fifteen and twenty-five years of age, at many stages of faith — and none. At times the tone is apologetic; then a devotional note is struck; and through most of the book runs an instructional thread, designed to give the sincere enquirer or young believer an over-all survey of Christian truth.

There may be one other sense in which this book is a stop-gap. I have been asked to write a book for some years, but the pressures of other work prevented me from doing so. I would love to develop some of the themes lightly touched upon here and, if the Lord allows me, now hope to do so. For example, I realise I have thrown out tantalising hints about questions which are matters of keen discussion among Christians today (I am excited, not depressed, by controversy — when it is engaged in the right spirit); I refer to such matters as believers' baptism, being filled with Holy Spirit and whether we shall be 'raptured' before the Great Tribulation. These questions certainly do not receive adequate treatment here, so please accept them simply as one man's statement of his conclusions after twenty-five years in a teaching ministry.

MILLMEAD CENTRE   DAVID PAWSON
GUILDFORD

Acknowledgments

No book is the work of one person. Even the Author of the Bible was helped by over forty men who turned his words into speech and print! He has also blessed me with the aid of a countless number who have helped me to be what I am and say what I have said.

A preacher picks up much of his material almost subconsciously, as he reads and listens to others. Unless he keeps a detailed card index (which I have never managed to do), tracing references can be difficult. So I dare say you will sometimes think as you read, 'He got that from . . .' — and you'll probably be right, though *he* may also have got it from someone else! I realise God's disapproval of plagiarising (Jeremiah 23:30) and ask forgiveness for any inadvertent 'borrowing'.

My father Professor Cecil Pawson, and my friend Pastor 'Bob' Morley, have been my preaching 'heroes'; the one for his passion and humanity and the other for his preparation and clarity. One always moved my heart and the other always excited my mind — but both preached for a verdict from the will. Their influence on me will be apparent to the discerning reader.

To many patient congregations (I have served fourteen as their pastor) I owe an incalculable debt. A shrewd observer, who has heard me preach 'at home' and 'away', has told me that I am at my best when I am preaching to those who know, love and are praying for me. That is profoundly true. These talks were drafted in private, but they were drawn out of me in public by a hungry family of brothers and sisters in the Lord. In particular, I would mention the fellowships at Gold Hill in Buckinghamshire and Millmead in Guildford, who have encouraged me more than they can ever realise.

Finally, and above all, to the Lord himself I offer my heart-felt gratitude for granting me the incredible privilege of 'breaking up his Word into small enough pieces for ordinary folk to digest' (as one dear old lady put it to me). To feed hungry bodies is a fulfilling task as a refugee worker and even a housewife knows; to feed hungry spirits is also rewarding. To be set free to devote so much time and energy to this is just another token of his goodness and mercy pursuing me all the days of my life.

The poem 'Teach me the Truth' by Frances Lockwood Green is reproduced by kind permission of Pageant Press Inc., New York.

Contents

1: Start Right Where You Are

The whole human race is feeling lonely. We have sent our astronauts 'out there', our radio telescopes have probed the depths of space, but they have found no one. So far as we know, we are alone in a vast, cold, lifeless universe.

A Swiss hotelier, Erich von Däniken, has made a fortune out of the loneliness of our age. His books — an incredible mixture of fact and fantasy — exploit man's need to know that there is someone or something 'out there'. In *The Chariot of the Gods* and *Return to the Stars* he propounds the theory that many years ago this tiny planet was visited by astronauts from outer space, and that the 'gods' of human history were in fact these visitors from other worlds. He admits that his ideas are the product of his own imagination and intuition, yet nine million copies of his books have been sold, in twenty-six languages.

How do we account for the appeal of such books? Or for the enormous success of the science fiction market? I believe the answer is to be found in this deep, inner loneliness of modern man, isolated — as he sees it — in an empty universe and calling out into the void, 'Is there anybody out there?' He longs to relate to someone or something beyond the limited confines of his own existence, but he sees and hears nothing in the great emptiness of space.

But that is not because there is no one there. The whole universe is alive with the life of God, but our unseeing eyes and unhearing ears fail to acknowledge the evidence. God fills and sustains his whole creation, yet modern man would rather believe the ridiculous fables and speculative nonsense of the science-fiction writers than accept anything as 'old-fashioned' and out of date as the concept of a personal God.

So we are going to look first of all at this whole idea of 'God' — what Christians mean by the word, and what is involved in believing that he exists.

The meaning of 'God'

When one of the first Russian cosmonauts returned from a space flight he said that he 'hadn't seen God out there'. On the other hand, one American astronaut, asked if he had met God in space answered, 'I would have done if I'd just stepped out of my space suit.' These are two contrasted understandings of the word 'God', rather than two contradictory answers to the same question.

I was speaking at a technical college when an English girl in her late teens interrupted to complain that I kept on using a word she could not understand. I assumed she was referring to some choice piece of theological jargon, but in fact she was referring to the word 'God'. 'What is that?' she asked, 'What does it mean?'

Another student told me that my use of the word 'God' clearly had a very different meaning from his. He explained that for him 'God' meant 'religious feelings' — his own, and other people's. I asked him whether his God would cease to exist if there were no people left to have these 'religious feelings', and he agreed that he would.

With all the different ideas about God which there are in the world, it may seem impossible to say anything certain or reliable about him. After all, no one has ever seen God — a fact that is inclined to make some people abandon the search for him before they have really begun it.

Yet it is necessary to start with something tangible and capable of examination, or we shall end up like the science fiction writers, passing off our ideas and theories as though they were facts. And for me one obvious place to start is with the universe itself. It is *there*, and its very existence poses a fundamental question: How did it get there? It seems strange that many people who say they want to find out about God ignore that very basic question.

There are four different answers on offer today. The first I find mind-boggling, but many people believe it so it cannot be ignored. They say the answer to the question 'How did the universe get there?' is that it did not. It is not really 'there' at all. The whole thing is a figment of the mind, an illusion. Matter simply does not exist.

The second answer, increasingly popular in recent years, is to say that the universe has always been there. It has changed, developed and evolved, but there was never a time when matter did not exist. This idea is at least as old as ancient Greece, and it has the merit of being a rational alternative to belief in creation, but modern research into the universe and its origins makes it an increasingly difficult position to defend. More and more scientists believe that the universe is not infinite either in space or time — that it had a beginning, and will have an end.

The third answer could be summed up in one word: chance. At some remote point in history nothing became something: by chance the ingredients occurred for a spontaneous 'creation'. Of course, this view presupposes the existence of the basic ingredients of matter, which seems to leave us where we were! Frankly, I think it takes more faith to be an atheist than to believe in God.

The fourth answer is the religious one, that this universe was *created*, and that the very fact of its existence is proof that there must be a power and an intelligence greater than the universe, which willed its existence. That 'power' and that intelligence is the being to whom we give the title 'God'.

Supposing you were exploring a desert region with four friends, and you stumbled across a fabulous palace. Each of your friends offered an explanation for its existence. 'It's only a mirage,' says the first — even after you have banged his head against its solid walls.

'It's always been there,' suggests the second. 'It's as old as the earth itself.'

'It put itself there,' offers the third, 'by a remarkable process of chance.'

'It was built by a famous architect,' says the fourth, 'I've met him myself.'

Which would *you* believe?

The Bible says that 'through the things he has made God's power and deity can be clearly seen' (Romans 1: 12). In other words, their existence is the proof of his existence. So a man who can look at the universe around him and say that there is no God has denied his own reason and talked himself out of the truth. Without opening the Bible at all, man can see some content to this word 'God'. Behind the things we can see there must be a power greater than those things. And men have always believed that that power is God.

It is true that at times this has expressed itself as belief in many 'gods', even in the 'heavenly bodies'. But if we go back through human history we find that in its beginnings man's religion was not a belief in many gods, but in one God who made everything. Only later did this degenerate into a belief in the plurality of gods, including rivers, mountains, the sun and the moon.

In Central Africa today there is one race which civilisation has largely passed by — the Pygmies. In them we can see many of the characteristics of man in his earliest, uncomplicated days. And the Pygmies believe in one God who made the world and everything in it. The first Maoris in New Zealand believed in a supreme creator, the origin of all being; his name was Io, and their story of how the world came to be bears a striking resemblance to Genesis. Now, alas, they believe in gods of war and peace, forest and agriculture, sea and sky.

Not that the Pygmies or the first Maoris required some unusual virtue or insight. Uncomplicated human eyes looking at the world as it is and uncomplicated minds thinking about it come to the conclusion that it was made by one God. We do not need the Bible to tell us that.

Nor do we need the Bible to tell us other things about God which we can deduce by using our eyes and our minds. It is possible to list some of these self-evident truths about God.

Firstly, he must be a God of tremendous *power*. Every tiny atom in the universe is packed with potential power. Man employs enormous power to hurl three-quarters of a ton of metal out of the earth's gravitational pull and into space. By comparison, can we begin to visualise the sort of power needed to get the earth itself into orbit, or pack the sun with the energy that fills our solar system? It is that power which is at God's disposal — inconceivable power.

Then, he must be a God of tremendous *intelligence*. After all, man prides himself on his intelligence because he can understand the universe in which he lives (though in fact, the more he finds out the less he seems to know). How much more intelligent must be the one who made it all.

Take one example: water. What amazing complexity is involved in this apparently simple substance which keeps our planet clean, fertile and cool. The tides move endlessly, washing our shores. Millions of gallons of water are caught up into the air every day and then dropped back on to the land, often from an altitude of several miles — and yet so gently that it sustains life without harming plants, animals or humans. That is the hallmark of intelligent planning. God is not only almighty, but intelligent.

He is also *imaginative*. Man tries to create variety, but often only succeeds in creating sameness. We have our artists and musicians, of course — people who use their sensitivity and flair to make or say something new and different. But God, the creator, is the supreme artist, whose imagination is at work in every corner of his creation, making an infinite variety of colour, shape and texture.

Then, God is *alone* — there is no other creative mind at work in our universe. In fact, it is just that: a *uni*-verse, not a *multi*-verse. However far we probe into space, we find that it runs on the same lines: gravity and velocity still apply. The laws of physics hold good. The inescapable conclusion is that there is one God, and only one, managing and holding together the universe he has made.

If I look one stage further, I am driven to yet another

conclusion about God: he is *personal*. That may seem a fairly sweeping conclusion to reach, simply on the basis of my experience of the world around me. And yet I believe it is completely logical.

As I look at the world, the highest, most advanced and apparently most significant creature is man, and personality, which distinguishes mankind from the animals, seems to be the most important quality in the universe. Can God, who created personality, be less than what he created?

Can I conceive him to be less than I am, one of his tiny, mortal creatures? He may be — indeed he *is* — much more than I am, but he cannot be less. He may be more than personal, but he cannot be less.

When I have reached that point, I set in train a series of consequences. The distinguishing marks of personality are such things as thinking, feeling, deciding, speaking and relating to other persons. It seems to follow, then, that God too must think, feel, decide, speak and relate to other persons.

So, without recourse to the Bible, I have already learnt a great deal about the nature of God, simply by sitting and thinking. Perhaps one of the reasons some people do not find God is that they are not prepared to do just this.

Nevertheless, sitting and thinking has its limitations. Having reached certain conclusions about the nature of God, how can I be sure that they are not merely delusions, projections of my own ideas or needs? How can I be sure that they correspond to reality?

The answer is that I cannot, if this search for truth is entirely one-sided. A finite creature can sit and think here on earth, and by reaching out with his brain can discover hints and notions of the kind of God there must be, but in the end there comes the point beyond which unaided human reason simply cannot go. Mere contemplation cannot get us beyond *ideas* which lack the kind of certainty and authority which changes lives and draws us to commitment.

But suppose the search is *not* one-sided. Suppose this personal God has spoken about himself. And suppose the record of what he has said about himself is still available. Then, surely, we would be in a position to confirm or reject the ideas about him which we arrived at simply by using our reasons.

Christians believe (as reason suggests) that God is a God who has spoken, who has voluntarily revealed the truth about himself. He has done it through human agents all down the centuries. He chose one small nation, Israel, to be the channel of his communication with mankind. From that one nation he chose a handful of men — the 'prophets' — to be his mouthpieces. And through them he has given the human race a picture of his own nature.

Does that picture coincide with what we have already deduced? Or does it conflict with what our brain tells us about the world around us? The amazing thing is that when we turn to the Bible, where the words of God's prophets are recorded for all time, we find that all the things indicated by reason are confirmed by revelation.

God tells us, for instance, that he is the *creator* of the universe. The very first words of the Bible tell us that: 'In the beginning God created'. He told Job, that outspoken Old Testament saint, that he had made and planned the world long before Job existed, so how dare he argue with God? 'Were you there?' God asks him 'Did you measure it out, survey it? Did you say to the seas, "This is to be your shore-line?"'
Job had no answer to that.

The Bible shows that God is infinitely *powerful*. The

world came into being at his word of command. Without any exaggeration one can say of God's creation, 'No sooner said than done!' God said, 'Let there be light' . . . and there was light. God said, 'Let the earth teem with life,' and it did. Every time he spoke, it happened. That, surely, is the mark of infinite power: he spoke, and it was.

But this God of power and might has also told us that he is *personal*. His intelligence, his imagination and his creativity express themselves through personality, so that he thinks, speak, feels, decides and relates to other beings in a personal way. All of this shines out through his own revelation of himself in the Bible, confirming, and, indeed, extending the ideas of him we have gleaned through the processes of reason.

It might at this point be objected that I am making God into nothing more than a glorified human being. Indeed, the same objection might be made to the Bible's portrait of him. A God who has personal qualities can easily be caricatured as an 'old man in the sky', no more than a cosmic superman, with human faults and failings to match.

The problem here lies in the question itself: 'Is God like us?' That is rather like asking if someone's father is like his son. It is the wrong way round. The Bible tells us that we are like God, 'made in his image and likeness.' But that is not to say that the greater is contained in the lesser and that he is like us. Of course, in many ways his personality *is* like ours (as we have seen). But in many important respects he is utterly unlike us — so unlike that our minds cannot grasp the difference.

There are five areas in which God is everlastingly different from us, and each is revealed in the Bible.

God is *spiritual*. He is a spirit, who cannot be seen, touched or located. We are tied to a particular location by our bodies, because material beings can only be in one place at a time. But a spiritual being is not limited in this way. God can be everywhere. He fills his creation.

It is very difficult for us to think of a God who cannot be apprehended by our normal senses of touch, sight, smell and hearing. God 'sees', but not with physical eyes. God 'hears', but not with physical ears. He allows us to use these material expressions because the functions of our bodies correspond in their results to the activities of God, but we must never make the mistake of assuming that this means that God has physical organs such as we have. He is spirit, and we have to relate to him spiritually.

Secondly, he is *omnipotent*. This does not mean that God can do anything, but that he can do anything he wants to do. When I was at school another boy came up to me and said, 'Can God do anything?'

Foolishly I fell into the trap and said, 'Yes, of course he can.'

'Can he tie a knot he can't undo?' Before I could think of an answer, he had walked away. It was years later that I came to realise that omnipotence means that God only has the ability to do anything that is compatible with himself. For example, God cannot lie and God cannot make mistakes.

Then, thirdly, God is *omniscient*: all-knowing. He knows the future as well as the past. Nothing is hidden from him, and there is nothing beyond his comprehension. Needless to say, this is an attribute that is unique to God.

Fourthly, as we have already seen, he is *omnipresent*: present everywhere.

A small boy asked his teacher if God was everywhere. On being told that he was, the boy asked 'Is God in my ink-well?' The teacher somewhat reluctantly agreed that that was so.

'Got him!' said the boy, clapping his hand over the ink-well.

He gets full marks for impudence, plus a few for initiative, but not many for theology. God is everywhere, but he cannot be limited to any one locality. He is not tied to place or space. If I were to ask, 'Lord, where in the universe are you?' he might answer, 'You've asked the wrong question. I'm not in the universe; the universe is in me!' As Paul put it to the intellectuals on Mars Hill in Athens, 'In God we live and move and have our being.'

So we have this strange paradox about God: he is near, so near that I am 'in him'; and he is far, in the sense of being greater and more sublime than anything I can imagine, 'dwelling in unapproachable light'. Some people complain that they have been looking for God and cannot find him — yet he is closer to them than their own breath. Other people speak of God as though he were the man next door, whereas he is infinitely greater than any being we can imagine. In fact, we need to hold these two ideas in balance — a God who is sublime and yet very near; greater than the universe itself, and yet even nearer to me than my own heart-beat.

Another attribute of God is that he is *eternal*, without beginning or end. The schoolboy who asks 'Who made God?' thinks he is being rather clever. In fact, his question is about at sensible as 'What is a square circle?' By definition, God simply exists. There cannot have been a time when he did not exist, and there can never be a time when he has ceased to exist. Otherwise, he would simply be a finite being like the rest of us, and not 'God' at all. In fact, his 'name' in the Bible, Jehovah, simply means 'I am'. For he is the permanent present tense.

Now of course it is hard for us to grasp this. In a sense, we cannot grasp it. Our minds are themselves finite, and simply cannot comprehend infinity. We tend to interpret it as meaning that God was 'always there', but even that is inadequate. God *exists*, in his own right, as part of his nature. 'From everlasting to everlasting I am God,' he says.

For every created being there are three tenses: was not (before it existed), is (now) and will not be (when it ceases to exist). But God describes himself as the one who 'was, and is, and is to come'. In other words, he is always there.

Perhaps one can sum up this picture of God by going back to that phrase about man being made 'in his image'. As we have already seen, that does not mean that God is made in our image, that he is totally 'like' us. But it does mean that we are 'like' him in some important respects.

However, if we fall into the error of thinking of God as 'like' us, then we shall be in danger of adopting an over-familiar attitude to him, which leads to irreverence, and destroys the sense of awe and wonder in our approach to him who is 'high above all'.

On the other hand, if we are obsessed with our 'unlikeness' to God, with his greatness and remoteness, then we shall not call him 'Father', and we shall never know the intimacy in prayer which is the privilege of his children.

Perhaps the only way to hold these two things in balance is to see them in Jesus Christ, the Son of God. For the greatest thing God ever did was to visit this planet as a human being, bringing the greatness and glory of eternity right into the daily life of mankind.

That is why Jesus could say, 'He who has seen me has seen the Father'.

Quite honestly, every other picture of him but the one provided by Jesus is inadequate. But when we find Jesus, we have found God.

2: Good God!

If you were to tell me that a man was going to call at my house tonight, and that he was six foot three in his socks, broad-shouldered, and with fists like a couple of tanks, I should be grateful for the information, but I would want to know a little more. What kind of a man is he? Is he peaceful or violent? Has he a short temper, or is he placid? Has he a grievance, or does he come with friendly intent? Only when I know that can I decide whether to lay out the welcome mat, or fix new bolts to the door.

In other words, a man's *attitudes* are, in some important respects, more significant than his *attributes*.

We have been looking at the attributes of God — his greatness, power, eternity, creativity, personality and so on. But in this chapter we turn to what is even more significant, his attitudes. How does he feel, what is he like, what motivates his actions?

I want to start with the moral attitude of God — his stance on moral issues. And at once there is a problem, for here is one of those areas where he is so *unlike* us as to make it almost impossible for us to comprehend him.

Let me illustrate this from one of Shakespeare's plays, *Measure for Measure*. The theme of this play is the dilemma of imperfect people trying to apply the laws of perfect morality. It is, as you know, about an apparently upright judge who distorts justice under the impact of a sudden temptation to lust. He declines to offer clemency to a young man guilty of the very sin he himself is contemplating. The play skilfully probes all the questions that this raises, and if Shakespeare could be said to have reached any conclusion about them it is probably summed up in the words of the good Duke near the end:

'They say best men are moulded out of faults,
And for the most become much more the better
For being a little bad.'

In other words, in an imperfect world we must learn to live with imperfection, tempering justice with mercy and being tolerant of the faults of others, knowing that we often have the same faults ourselves.

Now at one level that is reasonable enough. Jesus told us to forgive as we are forgiven, and he was scathing about the self-righteous judges of the woman taken in adultery. Of course we should temper justice towards others with mercy, and remember that 'in passing judgment on him you condemn yourself, because you, the judge, are doing the very same things', as Paul warned the Christians at Rome.

But on another level, this attitude of tolerance would, if carried to its logical conclusions, abolish all law, all courts, all police, all punishment . . . but not all crime or vice. It may seem tempting to argue that 'there is so much good in the worst of us, and so much bad in the best of us, that it ill behoves any of us to criticise the rest of us'. But that is really a recipe for moral anarchy.

It is more important to ask what God's attitude is in this matter, rather than reflect popular human philosophy. Is God strict or tolerant? Is he prepared to overlook my moral imperfections, as I am prepared to wink at those of my neighbour? Or does he operate on a different plane altogether? It is important to know, because the Bible says that one day God will examine and judge each of us, and we ought to be aware what his attitude on that day will be.

For God is *not* like us in his moral attitudes. 'To whom will you liken me?' he asks, anticipating the answer, 'No one'. He cannot be categorised in human terms (tolerant, stern, broad-minded, easy-going, harsh) because he does not work from human pre-suppositions.

For example, God is *Perfect*, and it is almost impossible for us to realise what that means, as we never encounter perfection in human existence. It is the universal experience of human nature that no one is perfect. All our virtues (as Shakespeare so superbly demonstrates over and over again in his plays) are accompanied by some vice that mars and distorts them. As soon as we manage to be humble we spoil it by being proud of it. Our sympathy for someone, which is a virtue, leads us to telling 'white' lies to protect them, which is a sin. The very concept of moral perfection is alien to all our thinking and all our experience. Yet the Bible tells us that God is absolutely and perfectly good.

He is absolutely *honest*. Among the short list of things God cannot do is to lie, or even tell a half-truth. If God says something it is true.

He is absolutely *fair*. Often people speak as though God had dealt in an unjust way with a person or a situation, but the Bible claims that 'the judge of all the earth is absolutely fair'. At the end of time, no one will have grounds for accusing God of injustice.

This absolute fairness of God enables the Christian to face some of the hardest questions calmly. 'What happens to babies who die — do they go to heaven?' I cannot claim to know, because the Bible does not tell me, but I know God well enough to be sure that

whatever he does with such babies will be absolutely
fair. 'What about those who die without having heard
about Jesus?' I cannot claim to know the answer, but I
know that whatever God does with them will be absolutely fair.

God is absolutely *pure*. No impure thought, intention,
word or action ever occurs to him.

He is absolutely *loyal*. Men break promises. Even
after our most solemn vows, as when a man or
woman stand in church and promise to love and cherish
each other until death, we break our promises and go
back on our pledged word. But when God says 'I will',
it is as good as done. He cannot deny himself. He keeps
his promises.

So God is perfect — a truth which may be somewhat
disguised for us by the debasing of the word 'good' in
modern English. 'God is good' is the most common
biblical statement of God's perfection, but we do not
normally use the word 'good' in this absolute sense.

When a rich young ruler came to Jesus he
asked, 'Good master, what must I do to have eternal
life?'

The answer Jesus gave is very revealing. 'Why do you
call *me* "good"?' he asked the young man. 'Only one
person is "good", and that is God.' Perhaps he hoped
that the man would follow up his original question by
arguing that as Jesus was undeniably good, he must be
nothing less than God. But he did not.

However, in his answer Jesus laid down a principle.
God alone is good, in this absolute sense. Of course, the
Bible refers to other people as 'good', in our normal,
comparative sense, but only God is good, absolutely
and utterly. Only God is perfect.

The Bible also uses the word 'righteous' to describe
God's moral attitude. It means not only to do right

but to *be* right — to act rightly because his nature is 'right'.

Similarly, the word 'holy' is used of God. As a word, it has an old-fashioned feel about it, but increasingly people are using it in songs of praise, giving God this title of perfection, 'holy, holy'.

Sometimes the Bible talks about God as 'light'. This refers not so much to physical light as to moral light, the idea that in the nature and character of God there is nothing to hide and there are no shadows. He alone is pure, blazing light.

However, it is the word 'perfect' that most clearly expresses God's moral purity for us. However well we may get to know God, the moment will never come when we find any flaw or defect in his character. God is perfect.

That statement raises a number of important implications about him. First of all, because he is morally perfect God has the right to define what is wrong — because he alone has an unbiassed judgment.

For imperfect beings like myself judgment is never unbiassed. Because of my own faults I shall almost inevitably fall into one of two extreme reactions to the moral failures of others. Either I shall excuse or condone them, or, at the opposite extreme, I shall condemn most severely in others the faults to which I know I am most prone. Either way, my judgment is distorted by my own sins.

But God, who has no sins, has the right to determine good and evil, right and wrong. It is natural to judge another by comparison with myself. When I do that, the result is a distortion of standards, because I fall short myself. But when God judges by comparison with himself, the result is perfect justice. It is that factor that makes my judgment false and God's judgment true.

The second implication of God's perfection is this —
he not only has the right to say what is wrong, but also
the right to punish the wrong-doer.

To go back to *Measure for Measure*, the basic theme
of that play is the impossibility of getting perfect justice
from imperfect people. No one, Shakespeare implies,
has the right to punish his fellow-men for faults he
himself shares. Now in practice that would lead to
anarchy, because no one would feel able to administer
any punishment at all. But the truth behind the argument is irrefutable. Perfect justice waits for the perfect
man to administer it.

And that is why the Bible reveals God, and God
alone, as the ultimate judge of all men. He has the right,
by his own nature, to define what is right and wrong,
and to punish those who do wrong.

All of this leads inevitably to another question. If
God has the right to punish evil, will he use it?

And that in turn leads to another question. What is it
like to deal with a *perfect* person? In ordinary human
experience, we never meet a morally perfect person, but
we do meet people who, in other spheres, have achieved
a kind of perfection.

I may play the guitar. If I meet a very fine guitarist —
someone whose playing is 'perfect' in comparison with
mine — my reaction to him will depend on his attitude
towards imperfect guitar players. If he is tolerant of my
ineptitude, we can get on well. But if he is arrogant,
superior and condemnatory, then I am destroyed. As
human beings, we rate 'tolerance' as the supreme virtue,
and we admire the person who can stretch his standards
low enough to include us.

And that is exactly what the human race hopes is
true of God. Although we realise he is perfect, yet we
hope that he will lower his standards so as to accept us,

as we are. We know he is against sin, but we hope that he will be tolerant of ours.

But there is no such God. However much we might like to visualise a kindly old man upstairs who pats us on the head and says 'Never mind, boys will be boys, we'll forgive and forget!', that is not the God of the Bible.

That super-tolerant God is simply a figment of the imagination, or a product of wishful thinking. The reason the God of the Bible is so unpopular is precisely this: that he will not in any way ignore the sins of the guilty. His forgiveness, when it is given, is a costly, sacrificial thing, not a matter of turning a blind eye to our faults.

For God is not only perfect, he is a perfectionist. That is to say, he is not content to be perfect himself. He also demands perfection in everyone else.

Perfectionists are not comfortable people to be with, because they are a constant rebuke to our imperfections. Henry Royce, co-founder of Rolls-Royce, was a perfectionist, which explains why his cars became a by-word for engineering accuracy. The story is told that one day he was walking around the factory and saw a man turning a piece on a lathe. After a while he put the piece on the pile of finished work, muttering, 'That'll do'. Henry Royce heard the remark, and dismissed the man on the spot. For him, the *name* of Rolls-Royce was at stake.

For God, the name of God is at stake, too. He cannot accept anything short of perfection — a fact that has to be accepted before one can truly appreciate the 'good news' to which we shall be turning later. There is no 'second best' with God.

For a perfectionist, everything has to be right. When God created the heavens and the earth, he surveyed what he had fashioned out of chaos and observed that it was 'very good'. And by that he meant, quite simply, 'as intended'. You may have had the experience of watching an artist or sculptor at work, and seeing him suddenly take the object and destroy it, crumpling the paper or pulping the clay. For you, the observer, it was an object of beauty. For the creator, who knew what was intended, it represented distortion and failure.

Josiah Wedgwood is a great name in English pottery. Wedgwood china achieved its unique status in a strange way. Josiah Wedgwood spent a good part of each day walking around his pottery works with a hammer destroying any piece that did not match up to his exacting standards.

God is certainly no less of a perfectionist than Josiah Wedgwood, and he has pledged himself to destroy everything in his creation that falls short of what he intended it to be. That is why it is really immaterial whether you have a great catalogue of sins to your discredit, or just the occasional moral flaw. God's verdict through the Bible — the Creator's judgment — is that 'all have sinned and fallen short of the glory of God'. And, like the scrupulous artist, God is bound to destroy that which is imperfect. Every part of this world bears God's stamp on it: 'Rejected'.

To those who object that a God of love would surely never destroy people simply because they are imperfect, it can only be replied that Sodom and Gomorrah, Babylon and Nineveh and the society of Noah's day indicate that he would, and does. There is nothing haphazard or arbitrary about this. God has set the standards, and then, by his actions, he maintains them.

'Who shall ascend the hill of the Lord? He who has nearly clean hands and an almost pure heart.' That would suit us as a standard. But it is not good enough for God. His standard is unequivocal: 'He who has clean hands and a pure heart.'

It may be objected that Jesus appeared less exacting in his demands. Indeed, some people try to contrast him with the God of the Old Testament. But I believe that the God who exists is the God of Jesus, and that Jesus himself is God. There can be no contradiction — and there is not.

In the Sermon on the Mount, for instance, Jesus demands perfection not only of behaviour but even of motive, intent and desire. He said it is better to go into heaven minus an eye or a foot than to go to hell with all your faculties. The more one studies the teaching of Jesus the more one finds 'perfectionist' teaching. Indeed, he ends the opening section of the Sermon on the Mount with the statement, 'Therefore be perfect, as my Father in heaven is perfect.' What is that but 'perfectionism'?

I believe Jesus is echoing there the Old Testament demand through Moses, 'Be ye holy, for I am holy.' That is the 'perfectionism' of God. It was echoed by Jesus, who not only spoke it in words, but demonstrated it in life.

Even his enemies conceded his perfection of character. In him the virtues were perfectly balanced and faults were entirely absent: Jesus could challenge his enemies to find a fault and they could not do it.

This leaves us with a rather grim situation, from a human viewpoint. Here we are, imperfect people in an imperfect world facing a God who is perfect and a Son of God who demands perfection of us. What chance have we got?

In view of this, many people have tried to ignore or play down the perfection of God. They evade the plain words of the Bible and project a God who compromises on evil, tolerates sin — and is even morally imperfect himself. But we simply cannot bring God down to our level, for reasons we have already set out.

So, what is to be done? If God cannot be reduced to our moral level, is there any way that we can be raised to his? We have already discussed the omnipotence of God — his ability to do anything he wants to that is consistent with his character. Clearly, then, he *can* make us perfect, and the fact is that the Bible through and through is not just saying God demands perfection, it says that God can share it with us!

God can make me perfect. He can take a sinner and turn him into a saint. He can take a person full of vices and faults, the worst of men, and begin a process of transformation.

Now there is a problem here, it must be admitted. The Bible calls Christians 'saints'. It may not make sense to an unbelieving world.

It appears not to have made sense to the translators of the Authorised Version of the Bible, who could not bring themselves to translate Paul's frequent phrase 'called saints' literally, and changed it to: 'called *to be* saints'. And one can see why. After all, even the best Christians are not perfect. Indeed, the more they grow in holiness the more aware they are of their imperfections. So how can it be said that they are saints, and that God can make a sinner 'perfect'. Surely that contradicts the plain evidence of my experience of life?

When my son used to play with his Meccano set, he would bolt together a few metal strips, pulleys and things. If I asked him what he was making, he said, 'It's a crane.' Now it did yet not look like a crane to my eyes. Frankly, it looked like a random assembly of nuts and bolts and strips of metal. But for him it was a crane, from the start — because in his mind was a picture of the crane he was making, and intended to finish.

So it is with God. He looks at the life of a person who is 'in his hand' and says, 'That's a saint.' The cynic says, 'He doesn't look like a saint to me. He's got faults. He's a hypocrite.' But God's answer is confident: 'I can see a saint, because I have begun to do something in that life and I'm not going to stop until my glory is in it.' God, in other words, is willing and able to make people perfect, and that is the only way for anyone to get to heaven. All that is imperfect will be destroyed, but those in God's hands are going to be perfect and live with him for ever in a perfect universe. Because God is a perfectionist he will not rest until he has got us right, and got the world right, too.

One question remains. If all this is true, why does God not do it for me, now? Why does he not just go ahead and make me good and holy, without delay? I have been asked that question many times, often in a tone of resentment, as though God should steam-roller the sinner into a state of perfection.

But forced goodness simply is not goodness. You cannot compel a man to be holy. That is why, before a life can be made perfect, God has to wait for one thing — our willingness to be made perfect.

And there's the rub. This willingness is, in biblical language, repentance, and repentance never came easily to anybody. But let us take a closer look at the word. We may find that we have undervalued it, or misunderstood its real meaning.

'Repentance' means much more than 'I'm sorry I got found out' or 'I'm sorry you've got to suffer as a result.' Essentially it means this: I am willing to let go of my imperfections, and to live without these things that spoil me. Now that goes deeper than it seems, and to turn that into a genuine prayer demands more than many people are willing to give. Those 'imperfections' have become part of me. If I let them go I am losing something of myself. There are also fears that a perfect life may be a dull one, that without a few indulgences and the occasional vice, boredom may set in. To be remade in God's image may lose us popular approval, or mark us out as misfits or oddities. It is really very costly to ask to be rid of our imperfections.

But God's call to us today is what it always was — Follow me, and I will make you . . . perfect. He longs to do it. But he will only do it when I am willing to let my imperfections go. I do not believe that decision leads to dullness or boredom, far from it. I believe it is the way to real life. The cul-de-sac is for those whose lives are going nowhere.

God says, 'Give me that old life — no matter how bad it has been, how low or corrupt. I will make it perfect — take away everything that spoils your character and damages your relationships – and give you eternal life.'

That life is not easy or comfortable, because God keeps on stirring it up, uncovering various imperfections, putting his finger on them, and dealing with them in a long process that leads to perfection in Christ.

3: The Course of True Love

The average family in Britain moves house once every six or seven years, and that is simply not long enough to put down effective social 'roots'. The pace of life is such that fashions in clothes, music, language and life-style change every four years, so that two young people five years apart in age find it difficult to communicate with each other, because they belong to different generations. People often feel they know television personalities better than they know the residents of the flat above.

If, as I believe, real life does not depend upon possessions, achievements or experiences, but upon relationships, then for many people in the modern world real life is barely attainable. This restless, changing, fly-by-night generation finds it more and more difficult to achieve deep and lasting relationships with other people.

It is this sense of deprivation, this failure to communicate with or relate to other people, that has led in recent years to various experiments in living. Many have tried living in communes in the hope that the smaller, more intimate community will make real relationships possible. At a less demanding level, the Christian musical presentation *Come Together* met a similar need. It encouraged people to reach out and *touch* someone else, in a spirit of fellowship. And that is what many of us need, because we are out of touch, unrelated to those around us. This is the cry of the lonely individual in a plastic world — let me touch you, let me be together with you, let me relate to you.

More specifically, of course, that is a cry for love, a cry echoed in a thousand pop songs. 'Love' is the one enduring vogue word of our day, but it has become a word so devoid of content that a whole cartoon series has been drawn on the theme 'Love is . . .' We want love, we demand love, but we are not sure what love is.

For our generation, then, the most striking phrase of the New Testament should have dramatic excitement: 'God is Love.' Unfortunately, this amazing statement excites little surprise even from Christians, who have been familiar with the words from childhood, but have become immune to the impact of them.

It is a revolutionary statement. Let there be no doubt about that. It does not say, as it well might, that 'God has loved' or that 'God is loving', but that God *is* love. So far as I know, there is not another religion in the world that makes a claim like that. There has been no other god nor any religious leader of whom it is said that he *is* love. We may say that a person loves, or is loving, but the claim that he is love itself is exclusive to the God and Father of our Lord Jesus Christ.

Perhaps the Bible's statement might have more impact to a modern reader if it were paraphrased in a contemporary idiom. 'God is togetherness' might convey the shock better, for it includes the idea that God must be more than one person. You cannot be together on your own.

Now we know that God is one, and yet he must be more than one person if he is and has always been love. God's character, like his nature, is eternal, so it must be that before there was a universe and before there were any human beings to love, God was love, togetherness, harmony, peace.

But with whom did he express these 'social' character-istics? The answer, of course, as we have already dis-covered, is that God is not a simple unity.

An illustration may help, provided it is not pushed too far — I am using human imagery to express a concept that has no human parallel. If we think of God as a family, we can see how there could be an experience of love, harmony and peace between the Persons who make up that family. Incidentally, the Bible says that every family on earth is 'named after' God, but the divine 'family' is closer than anything we can imagine — its members actually share each other's nature.

But here is the heart of love: the Father always loved the Son, the Son always loved the Father, and the Father and the Son always loved the Spirit. Here was and is a triangular relationship of perfect love, without any preference or envy.

Sometimes we may doubt whether there is such a thing as genuine, disinterested love. We may have had bad experiences ourselves, in our childhood or in later life, and become cynical about the very possibility. But the truth is that at the heart of the universe, in its Creator, there is real, genuine and disinterested love — there always has been, and there always will be.

Let us take this a step further. For instance, is there any chance of my breaking into that triangle of love? Can I take the hands of Father and Son and say, 'Let me into this relationship?'

The truth is even better than that possibility, for the Father and the Son have already stretched out their hands and said 'We want you to share this'. Right from the opening chapters of the Bible there is this clear teaching — God is 'togetherness'. Indeed, a literal translation of the first five words of the Bible would be, 'In the beginning Gods (plural noun) created (singular verb) ... ' Later the same thing occurs, 'God said let *us* make man in *our* image'. It is as though God were saying that the love and unity enjoyed from eternity by the three Persons of the God-head were now to be available more widely. I suppose God created men because he wanted to bring more persons into the circle of his love.

And that is a hallmark of love. True love is never selfish, exclusive or narrow. It always wants to reach out and embrace others. Someone has said that real love is not sitting looking into each other's eyes the whole time, but looking out in the same direction together.

So it is entirely consistent that God should want to widen the family, and have many more sons to follow the one he already had. Indeed, Christ was to be the firstborn of many sons he would bring to glory and into the family.

So within the one God there are three conscious personalities whose minds think as one, whose wills act as one and who are in a relationship of perfect harmony with each other. This relationship is so close that if you pray to one you feel you are talking to the other two as well.

Sometimes people ask, 'Should I pray to the Father or to Jesus, the Son?' The answer has to be that the Christian can pray to whichever one he chooses and to whoever it seems natural to pray at that moment; and such is their unity that each member of the Trinity is immediately involved. Personally, I get the same reaction, the same feeling, when I am praying, which-ever 'member' of the Godhead I am addressing.

Probably the nearest human experience can get to this unity is the 'perfect' marriage, where (in the Bible's words) two become one, so that they are not referred to separately any longer, but are described as 'the Browns' or 'the Joneses'. That is a double unity, but God, of course, is a triple unity, a tri-unity or 'trinity', as we usually say. No one can fully understand the Trinity, but then creatures can hardly expect to comprehend their Creator. This is simply a point where we have to acknowledge that God is so utterly unlike anything we can comprehend that we can only bow in 'wonder, love and praise'.

We can now move on to a second statement. God is love, and God *loves us*. The second would be meaningless without the first, but taken together they reveal that God, having created us, wants to draw us into the circle of his love.

But this in itself is an almost incredible statement — that the God who shaped the universe and put the stars in space loves me as though I were the only person in the world. Some of our difficulties in accepting this idea arise from misunderstandings and even delusions about the nature of the love of God. Basically these are expressed in two common questions: why does God love us? and how does God love us?

To take the first question, many people ask, Why does God love *me*? A very common misunderstanding lies behind that question, for it implies that God must need to find something attractive or lovable in me before he can be said to love me. Strangely enough, what lies behind this apparently modest notion (what is there in me for God to love?) is simply human pride. We assume that God's love is like ours, which is drawn out by something we find attractive, commendable or lovable in another person. But nothing could be further from the truth. When God looks into my heart he sees not an attractive person, but an ugly one; not someone holy, like himself, but someone very far from holy. If we could see ourselves as God sees us, we would never come to the mistaken conclusion that we can earn, deserve or attract God's love. In other words, he does not love us because we are lovable; far from it.

We may find a clue to the wider question by looking at a more specific instance. Instead of 'Why does God love me?' let us ask 'Why did God choose the Jews?' Out of all the world he chose this one nation of people to reveal his salvation through his Son ... but why the Jews? Why not the Assyrians, the Greeks, the Ethiopians or the Chinese? Are the Jews more attractive, more reliable, more religious? Have they some unique racial qualities denied to all the other nations? I do not think so.

God gives his reason for choosing the Jews in chapter seven of Deuteronomy. 'Do you think I love you because you are a greater nation than all the others? No, I love you *because I love you*.' That is the answer; and it lies not in them at all, but in him.

God loves me not because I am lovable but because he is love. And his love, as we have seen, is not like our love. In fact, only the Greeks have a word for it! In the Greek of New Testament times there were several words for love, covering things like sexual love, affection, friendship and so on. But there was one word, *agape*, which was used of the love that one could have for a person who has nothing within themselves to attract that love. Needless to say, it was a word that was seldom employed.

But the New Testament writers rescued it from oblivion. It was precisely the right word to express the love of God — a love which begins in the lover and goes on to create in the loved one all the attractive and lovable qualities that were not there to begin with. It is, of course, very humbling to be told that there is nothing lovable about us as we are, but that is the truth about the matter. We are not just 'stray sheep' for whom God is patiently searching, but rebels with weapons in our hands defying our Creator. And yet he loves us.

Jesus described human love as 'loving those who love you', and its finest expression in the man who 'lays down his life for his friend'. But, as Paul puts it, 'God commends his love towards us in that *while we were yet sinners* Christ died for us.' There is the contrast between God's love and human love at its very best.

This brings us to the second question: *how* does God love us? Here again we have to clear away the debris of misunderstanding in order to get at the truth. The general notion of God's love is that it is a kind of sentimental sympathy for our plight, a love which turns a blind eye to our shortcomings and simply wants us to be happy.

I once knew a family in which the children were never punished. No matter what they did, from smashing windows to painting the cat green, was excused as childish exuberance or legitimate self-expression. I must admit at times I envied them. But what those parents were offering their children was not love so much as sentimental indulgence. Yet that is what many people think God offers us!

If it were true that the love of God was simply a matter of sentiment and softness, then all that we have already argued about the perfection and holiness of God would be totally undermined. That kind of 'love' would be quite incompatible with God's stated determination to eradicate from his universe all that corrupts and defiles it.

It is often argued by well-meaning people that a God of love would never exclude anyone from heaven.

Surely, they say, if you believe in the love of God you cannot also believe in ideas of hell or judgment?

But this is not the 'love of God' we read of in the Bible. If God overlooked my sin he would not be showing real love, but unconcern. *Because* he loves me, and because his love is pure and holy, he did something far more costly than simply to overlook my sin. He gave his Son to die for it. He paid the price, which makes sin the most expensive commodity in the world. It is expensive for the sinner: it costs him eternal life. It is expensive for God; it cost him the death on the cross of his Son Jesus.

Sin has to be paid for, because this is a moral universe, where God reigns — and he is perfect, just and true. If sin does not matter, then anarchy sits on the throne of the universe. The choice is as stark as that.

Dr. Billy Graham puts it like this. 'Don't make the mistake of thinking because God is love everything is going to be sweet, beautiful and happy, and that no-one will be punished for his sins. God's holiness demands that all sin must be punished, but God's love provided the cross of Jesus by which man can have forgiveness and cleansing.'

There is the divine dilemma. God hated sin but he loved sinners. God wanted to destroy sin, but he wished to save the sinner who committed it. How could he separate the two? Even before the first man committed the first sin, God knew the answer, and he also knew what that answer would cost: the sacrifice of his Son.

There can be no Christianity without a cross, and no true relationship with God that does not begin beneath its shadow. That is the cost of our forgiveness.

It is a cost that has been borne entirely by God. We can appreciate something of the suffering of Jesus —

the physical agony of crucifixion under a hot sun; the mental agony of being executed for crimes he did not commit; the spiritual agony of being cut off from his own Father, of going through hell itself. But can we also appreciate the suffering of the Father? He was not an indifferent spectator of his Son's sufferings for mankind. Far from it. Christ's agony was the agony of the God-head.

I read recently a novel called *The Gadfly*, written in 1897 by E. L. Voynitch. It is an extraordinary book with a breath-taking climax. A Roman Catholic priest, Montinelli, is the father of an illegitimate boy who becomes a rebel when he learns about this relationship. Montinelli advances in the Church and ultimately becomes a cardinal in an Italian city. The boy takes to political agitation and eventually leads a group of terrorists who are trying to overthrow the State. Arrested by the police in his father's city, he is sentenced to death and the cardinal — who does not know his identity — is given the opportunity to exercise clemency. He visits the boy in his cell and discovers it is his own son, but for the sake of the people he decides he cannot prevent the execution.

On the Sunday after his son has been shot by a firing squad the cardinal speaks in the cathedral just after communion at the mass. 'It is written in the Gospel of John,' he says, 'that "God so loved the world that he gave his only begotten son that the world through him might be saved". This is the festival of the body and blood of the victim who was slain for your salvation, the Lamb of God "who taketh away the sin of the world", the Son of God who died for your transgressions. And you are assembled here in solemn festival array to eat of the sacrifice that was given for you and render thanks for this great mercy. And I know this morning when you came to share the banquet — to eat of the body of the Victim — your hearts were filled with joy when you remembered the passion of God the Son, who died that you might be saved.

'But tell me, which among you has ever thought of that other passion, the passion of God the Father, who gave his Son to be crucified? Which of you has remembered the agony of God the Father when he bent from his throne in the heavens above and looked down upon Calvary?

'I have watched you today, my people, as you walked in your ranks in solemn procession, and I have seen that your hearts are glad within you for the remission of sins and that you rejoice in your salvation. Yet I pray you consider at what price this salvation was bought. Surely it is very precious and the price of it is above rubies. It is the price of blood.'

The story goes on to tell how the cardinal then went mad. He simply could not take the agony of the choice he had to make as a father between killing his own son and saving his people. Within a few days he was dead. A human heart simply could not cope with that kind of choice.

God shared the agony of Calvary. The Father put your sins and mine on his own Son to save his people. That is the measure of his love.

Love is measured not so much in what it feels as in what it does: the suffering it is prepared to face, the pain it is prepared to accept. And it is suffering and pain that is the measure of God's love.

Indeed, it does not finish at the cross. There the guilt of sin was dealt with, but God goes on pouring his love into our lives to sustain us in the forgiven life. Not only did Jesus take my place in his death, he takes my place in life, too. So Jesus died in my place and lives in my place, and God's love begins to remould me until I am perfect, fit for glory.

God loves us in our sin not by letting us off but by providing his Son to die for us. It is a gesture of total love, for which the New Testament coins a special word, 'grace'. It means a love that is not deserved and cannot be earned, a love that is simply poured out at the expense of the giver. Someone defined it as *G*od's *R*iches *A*t *C*hrist's *E*xpense. There simply is nothing to pay. God has done it all. No wonder it is called 'amazing grace' — the best of all news about God. He is great. He is good. But best of all, he is *gracious*.

4: Naked Ape or Fallen Angel?

Someone once rang me in the early hours of the morning with a burning question, *'Who am I?'* The caller knew his own name and address, of course. He was not suffering from amnesia. Yet he was unsure of his identity. And in that he is a living, breathing symptom of the age we live in.

Who am I? What are we? What is man? There are thousands of young people wandering the world today, hitch-hiking across continents, taking other kinds of 'trips' with drugs, all in search of the answers to those questions. They, and the rest of us, are offered plenty of answers, too — most of which fall into two extreme and diametrically opposed groups.

On the one hand there are those who say that man is an animal, no more and no less. This idea is propagated in books like *The Naked Ape* by Desmond Morris, which trace our social behaviour back to the jungle. Since Charles Darwin popularised the theory of evolution — a theory which had been around, in one form or another, at least as far back as Aristotle — we have suffered from the obsession that our society is a jungle in which the fittest will survive through struggle. But if men are just highly developed animals, they cannot be blamed for acting as though they lived in a jungle. Men's minds have been brainwashed with the idea that they are no more than intelligent animals, and it could be argued that the bestiality of the twentieth century flows directly from that. But the Christian does not and cannot believe that man is an animal. It is a libel on God, in whose image he was created.

At the other extreme we are faced with the idea that man is now his own god. The argument runs along these lines: man has come of age; he can now do for himself what once he used to pray for; he now knows for himself what once he could only accept by faith. He can now live without outside help.

As human knowledge increases — and ninety per cent of all the scientists of history are alive today, so that the increase is very fast indeed — the point approaches at which man will become convinced of his own omniscience and finally dismiss the notion of divine omniscience.

Man is becoming convinced of his own omnipotence, too. My grandfather would have laughed at the thought of being able to sit in his own living room and watch events in Japan as they happened. But even that would not stagger him as much as the idea of transplanting parts of the human body. It is that kind of thing that gives modern man the idea that nothing is beyond his power.

In a limited sense, he has even achieved omnipresence. God is everywhere at once. Man cannot quite equal that, but he can be everywhere very quickly. A hundred years ago we crawled around like ants on this planet. Now even the planet cannot confine us. We have been to the moon, and may well one day go to Mars, or beyond. Omnipresent, omnipotent, omniscient: it is easy to see how man has come to see himself as god.

However, there is one attribute of God that man has not been able to achieve, though he desperately desires it: eternity. We have managed to stretch the average human life-span by a few years, but we are very far from achieving immortality on earth. Scientists look for the secret of life and try to eliminate one by one the factors that cause death, but still death remains un-defeated, despite all man's ingenuity and medical skill.

Nevertheless, it is popularly supposed that this problem, with all others, will be solved in due course, and then the strange contradiction of man the animal and man the god will be complete. Between those two positions most people hover, sometimes emphasising man's animal qualities, and sometimes his divine ones. The Christian watches the argument: is man an animal, or is he god? His answer is — neither. He has affinities with both, but he is to be identified with neither.

As unique creatures on God's planet we live in the same environment as the animals. Our bodies and physical systems are like theirs, and like them we eventu-ally return to dust. And as unique creatures of God we also have affinities with him: we are 'made in his image'. But in both cases there are enormous, ineradicable distinctions as well. We are neither animals nor gods.

The dignity of man
Man's dignity, given him by God, helps to distinguish him from the animals, and gives him his unique place in the hierarchy of creation: not low down, among the animals, and not at the top, where God is; but, in fact, number three in the charts, 'a little lower than the angels'.

He is above the animals, even though he has so much in common with them. When we took the children to the zoo they liked best of all to watch the chimpanzees and orangutans, mainly because their behaviour was so 'human'. In fact, watching them it was only natural to ask what precisely is the difference between these apparently 'intelligent' mammals and primitive or uncivilised human beings. It was thought at one time that the decisive difference was that man made and used tools, but a few years ago a young Christian woman who lived for a time with a family of chimpanzees in Africa discovered that they could and did make and use tools. Others have argued that man uses fire, or that he laughs and animals do not. But the real difference is rather more surprising. Man *prays*.

From the beginning of the human race there are traces of this religious instinct — the feeling that man can and should reach out from the material world to the spiritual one. But no one has ever found any trace anywhere of an animal seeking to relate to an invisible power that made the universe. Over against that, there is something in man that draws him out beyond the natural world to worship and pray.

In early burial customs there is evidence of a primitive belief in life beyond death, and all through man's history there are traces of his religious beliefs and worship, however misguided or primitive they may have been. It is this religious instinct that sets man apart among the creatures: he knows his place in the universe; he recognises that he is not at the top of the hierarchy of creation but that there is above him a power which he ought to reverence and before which he ought to bow.

The Bible sets it out in this way. When God had made the universe, the plants and the animals, he then proceeded to a further, special act of creation: he made man. 'Let us make man,' he said, 'in our own image.'

It is quite impossible to plumb the depths of that statement, but it is safe to say that it is at the very heart of the truth of the universe. I cannot define it, but I can project two illustrations which help to draw out the meaning of the word 'image'.

There is, firstly, the 'image' that can be found on a coin — the head of the monarch or president. Whatever you do with the coin, the image remains; and whatever you do to the monarch, the image remains as well. The image, in other words, is independent of its original. Kings and queens may come and go, but long after they are dead their image remains and survives on the coins minted under their authority.

Then, secondly, there is the 'image' you can see in a mirror, which only survives while the object remains in the correct physical relationship to the mirror. It has no independent existence. It can reflect, but it cannot survive on its own.

I believe that the statement that man is made 'in the image of God' covers both these meanings — and probably much more. There is a sense in which certain capacities that I have as a human being made in God's image are mine and will survive as long as I do: the capacity to communicate, the capacity for self-determination and for dominion. But there is also an 'image' which I can lose, an image which depends utterly on my being in a face-to-face relationship with God.

So I do not think it is fanciful to claim, as I believe the Bible does, that you cannot be truly human unless you are in fellowship with God. It is the loss of that relationship that has dehumanised modern man and distorted the divine image in him and in his society.

Nevertheless, man, made in God's image, *is* above the animals. That is his place in the order of creation. But, as I have suggested already, he is not second to God in the divine order, but third. Between man and God comes an order of beings we often overlook — the angels.

Science fiction is always asking frantically, 'Is there intelligent life anywhere else in the universe — life that is different and apart from the human race?' For centuries the Bible has been saying 'Yes, there is'. There *is* intelligent life 'elsewhere', and it is superior to us. The angels are superior to humans in intelligence, beauty and power.

Our place is just below them — 'a little lower than the angels', as the psalmist puts it. And our calling is to accept and fulfil our place. Only misery and disappointment can ensue for those who step out of the divinely ordered patterns of things.

Some people step out of it by bowing down to trees, hills and animals, giving them a place reserved for God and his angels, worshipping the creature instead of the Creator. More frequently, man rejects God's order by seeking to promote himself to a place that is not his, ascribing to himself power, authority and judgment that are in fact reserved for God. Both attitudes are wrong, and both lead to disaster.

The depravity of man

However, the 'disaster' of the human race goes even further back than man's inability to accept his proper place in the created order, though that was an element in his original rebellion. As we look at the world around us, it is obvious that something has gone terribly wrong. One third — the West — is tottering under anarchic pressures, its way of life threatened by corruption and decadence. Another third — the East — lies in bondage to totalitarian regimes, deprived of liberty and virtually dehumanised. The other third — the so-called 'third world' — scrambles to find enough to feed its rapidly growing population . . . and many go short. Something is terribly and basically wrong.

In the nineteenth century there was a general air of optimism. One British prime minister fought an election on the slogan 'Up and up and up, and on and on and on'. What empty complacency that seems, from our perspective! Two world wars and the ensuing madness have shattered such illusions. What has gone wrong?

The Bible gives the answer to that question. Things went wrong from the very beginning of the human race — indeed, even before that. People often ask, 'Where did evil come from? Who invented it?' The answer is that neither God nor man 'invented' evil; it started among the angels. A group of angels set themselves up against God. 'There was war in heaven', with Lucifer as the leader of the rebels — Lucifer who, after his expulsion from heaven, is called Satan. God did not create evil; neither did man. But God made us free to be evil (and presumably the angels as well). Evil does not exist apart from evil beings, but an evil angelic being took the opportunity to sow the seed of temptation in the mind of the first human beings, creatures of God.

The temptation was a basic one: 'You could be like God'. First the woman and then the man allowed themselves to dwell on the idea of their own independence of God. They began to question God's rules, to ask why they should be his tenants on the earth, rather than its landlords.

And their eventual disobedience set in train those horrible consequences with which all mankind is only too familiar — physical death (which was not part of God's original plan for mankind); and spiritual death, which cuts us off from God. Both are universal. From the moment of birth we are doomed to die. And from the moment of birth we are all spiritually dead. When the psalmist cries, 'In sin did my mother conceive me', he did not mean that he was illegitimate, nor that sexual intercourse was evil, but that the congenital disease of sin is part of human nature since the fall. None of us can dissociate himself from what has happened to our race; each one of us is part of the whole mess.

Christians believe in the 'universal depravity' of man. What that rather daunting phrase means is what we have just seen, that there is not a human being born who is not a sinner, and what he is by nature, he soon confirms by choice. He does things which he knows are wrong, and by doing them he adds to the world's troubles rather than reduces them.

Many people would reject this idea entirely. For them, man is innately good. They believe in 'original virtue' rather than 'original sin'. They point to all the good and kind people around them, and perhaps to their own code of conduct, and contrast this with what seems to be the dreary concentration of the Bible and Christianity on the element of evil. Surely this is a depressing diagnosis, a counsel of despair?

The truth is that it generally pays to be 'nice'. It is in the interests of society as a whole to have 'nice' people around — good, moral, law-abiding people. So the pressure from the social order is for us to appear nice rather than nasty. Perhaps best of all is to live in a state of anaesthetised neutrality, where the citizen is neither really good nor really bad, but keeps the law, pays his taxes, performs his routine work in a predictable fashion, is quiet, orderly and well-mannered, neither disturbingly vicious nor virtuous, just *nice*.

After all, it is not in the interests of a well-ordered society to have too many of its members highly energetic, dynamic or creative. Such qualities are dangerously unpredictable, and may well get out of control. For society to be safe it needs not artists, but assemblers;

not prophets, but priests; not poets but men who will write what is expected of them. Yet it is only in the creativity, energy and dynamism of man that our society has any hope of improvement, for each of these is a gift of God, part of the divine image.

It is in these divine powers that we can see most clearly the depravity of man. Given god-like powers, how does he wield them? For good? For mankind's benefit? For peace and love and freedom? It is when we take a cool look at what man has done with his creative potential that we see most clearly how misleading is the concept of original innocence. With that potential — with his god-like powers — man has fashioned his weapons of exploitation and subjugation, until today he possesses the means of total and final destruction. Man has always been the chief architect of his own destruction. 'People' may be 'nice', but man is always evil.

The apostle Paul knew the heart of man, and his own heart. He wrote, 'The good that I would I do not; the evil that I would not, that I do.' In that one sentence I believe he summed up the dilemma and the depravity of man. Made for God and for good, his fallen nature nevertheless always pulls him downwards. He never reaches the heights he knows to be there.

The destiny of man

So what is the destiny of the human race? Where does all this lead? My answer in two words is, utter disaster. I can see no hope for the human race in itself. It is impossible for me to be other than a sheer pessimist as regards the future course of human civilisation. I believe the destiny of our race is to perish: not to die and cease to be, but to 'perish' in the biblical meaning of the word, to cease to be human, to be cut off from

God, to become totally dehumanised. We can see it happening all around us, and the process will accelerate. Jesus said the position would get worse and worse until the end of the age.

But there will be an end. If I stopped at this picture of total gloom I would be unfair to what the Bible says about the final destiny of man. God does care, and he is not standing idly by while his creatures perish. He may have written off the planet on which we live, and the world order of which we are so unjustifiably proud, but he has not written off mankind.

He has planned to create a new humanity, to start afresh with a new order of mankind in a new world of justice and righteousness. But, in his love and mercy, he decided to fashion the new humanity out of the old people — to take us and make us new. But, as ever, God does not deal with 'man', but with *men*. He says, 'I want *you* to be a new human being for me.' And through Christ, who came to this earth to save men from perishing, he has made it possible. 'If any man is in Christ, he is a new creature.'

The way this can come about is the very opposite of the devil's way. The devil tempted man by offering him a chance to advance himself, to climb up the ladder and become 'like God'. But God requires the very opposite. We are to climb down the ladder, right to the bottom, and there we are to admit that we have done things that offend against God's laws and standards, that we are sinners not only by nature but in practice. And then, when we have humbled ourselves, and thrown ourselves on his mercy in Christ, he will lift us up ... not just to where we were, but to an even higher place above the angels. This new humanity in Christ is destined for a place next to God himself. What a destiny!

So the way up is the way down. Proud, misguided

man, trying desperately to climb up among the gods, has to start again, from the bottom. He has to recognise that there is no hope for him unless he is re-made by God. The human qualities that have put him above the animals cannot survive without a relationship with the God who gave them in the first place. There is this stark choice: to perish, or to start again; slowly to lose your humanity, or to find in Christ that you have become fully human for the first time.

5: Who On Earth Was He?

Have you ever had the experience of being in a group of people who are talking about a friend of yours? Someone says something which you know to be downright false or misleading. Suddenly you are faced with a direct choice. Do you keep quiet, not revealing that you know the person who is being maligned? Or do you interrupt and say, 'Look, I know this person, and I think you've got the wrong end of the stick — he's not like that at all.'

I constantly get that feeling when I hear people talking about Jesus. Time and time again I want to interrupt and say, 'That's not the Jesus I know.' I am glad that they are talking about Jesus — and never in my twenty-five years as a minister have people talked as much or as freely about him as they do today — but one longs that they should talk about the *real* Jesus. His name is frequently in our ears: on television and radio, in films and on 'pop' records. But over and over again what is said about him makes me want to object that this is not the Jesus I know from the Bible: and there is no other Jesus. People who have never bothered even to read the Gospels through — the work of a few hours — trot out dogmatic assertions about what he was or was not like. And many of their ideas are the opposite of the facts about him.

For instance, we are often told that Jesus always looked for the good in people and turned a blind eye to the evil in them. But that simply is not so. In fact, he was always putting his finger on the evil and damaging things in people's lives. This was what he did with the woman he met at the well — gently, lovingly but devastatingly he exposed her immorality and offered her a new and better life. He called the hypocritical religious leaders of his day 'white sepulchres'. These were hardly the actions of a man who 'always looked for the good in people and turned a blind eye to the evil in them'.

Then we are told that Jesus 'trusted' everybody, as we should too. But when I open the Gospels I find it recorded that 'he would not trust himself to any man, because he knew what was in man' (John 2: 24f.).

It is also argued that Jesus only talked about the love of God, and would not have agreed with preachers who go on about judgment and hell. Yet almost every parable he told was about judgment, and it is from the lips of Jesus himself that we get our doctrine of hell: nobody else in the entire Bible says much about it!

There have been assertions, too, about the character and personality of Jesus. Several years ago a bishop implied that Jesus may well have been homosexual. Since then other things have been said or suggested about him, including a pornographic Danish film on his alleged sexual activities. Those responsible for these statements may not have to answer a writ for libel before a human court, but one day they will answer for them in the court of heaven.

The vital thing is to get away from human speculation about Jesus, of whatever kind or however motivated, and re-assert the Jesus of the Gospels — the only true, reliable and authentic Jesus that there is. It is not only

unbelievers and the ignorant who have distorted the
picture of Jesus. Christians must take their share of the
blame. After all, if people look at us as Christians —
Christ's men and women — and at the Church as the
body of Christ, they can hardly be blamed for getting
the impression that Jesus must have been rather an
anaemic, ineffective sort of person.

Yet the true picture is readily available. His very
words and actions, reported by eye-witnesses, are there
in the New Testament for anyone who takes the trouble
to read it. All the distortions and man-made ideas
about Jesus can be corrected by this. So I would like
to summarise the evidence of the Bible about Jesus, to
put the record straight and to make it possible for us to
respond to the Person he really is, rather than the image
men have made of him.

The first thing one has to say about the Jesus of the
Gospels is that there can be no doubt that he was a *real*
human being. He had a body like ours: he needed rest,
he became hungry and thirsty, he knew pain and
discomfort. He had a mind like ours: he had to learn
to read and write, he had a sense of humour, he employed logic and reason. He had a spirit like ours: he
felt the need to pray, and he joined in public worship
every Sabbath at the synagogue. We are dealing with a
real man, human in body, mind and spirit — at his
trial Pilate could point at him and say, 'Behold the man',
Jesus was the representative man, showing human life
at its fullest and best. Even those who cannot believe
that he is divine are drawn to this person. Mahatma
Gandhi and Dostoievsky are two among countless
thousands of every race and culture who have looked at
the life of Jesus and said, 'That is how human life
ought to be lived.' There is something beautiful and
irresistible in this man.

But if we say that Jesus was a man 'like us', we ought to go on to ask, 'Like which of us?' When I examine his life I find in fact that he was not born as I was born, he did not live as I live nor do things as I do them, and he did not die as I die. There is a dimension to the life of Jesus that distinguished him as a very *remarkable* person indeed.

Let me take three events in the first thirty years of his life to indicate the uniqueness of Jesus of Nazareth.

First, there was his birth. In one sense this was quite normal. He came from his mother's womb in the usual painful way. But the origin of that birth was not normal. His conception was not the result of a man and a woman making love. His was a virgin birth.

Such births are not totally unknown, of course. Some plants and simple animals have the capacity to reproduce themselves without any process of fertilisation, but until recently it was thought impossible for this to happen to human beings. However, a scientific investigation of cases where it was claimed women who were virgins had given birth to babies has left a small number of cases — perhaps five or six — where it seemed possible that the claim was true, and that the female ovum had begun to divide spontaneously and eventually produce a baby. But in every one of these cases the baby was a girl, because the egg is female. So if the virgin Mary's baby was no more than a natural, if rare, freak, the child could not possibly have been a male ... but Jesus was. His birth, then, was totally unique.

Of his boyhood we know very little, but the one incident that is recorded is enough to demonstrate how unusual it was. When he was twelve he was taken by Joseph and Mary to the temple in Jerusalem for the ceremony which every Jewish boy undergoes at that age, his 'barmitzvah'. This marks the point at which he becomes a man, legally a partner in his father's business. On the way home to Nazareth after the ceremony, Jesus went missing. He should have been with his father, now that he was a 'man' (the men and women travelled separately), but Joseph assumed he was with his mother. His absence was discovered during the overnight stop, and Joseph and Mary went back to Jerusalem to look for him. They found him in the temple, engaging in learned conversation with the rabbis there. Mary, naturally upset, chided him.

'We've been worried stiff — *your father* and I have been searching for you everywhere.'

The young man's reply was simple, but startling. 'Didn't you know that I would be about *my father's* business?'

At that point Mary realised, perhaps with a shock, that Jesus knew perfectly well that Joseph was not his father, and that God was, that he had done something unique in the womb of that young teenage girl — something that had never happened before and has never happened since.

The third unique incident was the baptism of Jesus. I have never heard of any other baptism at which there was an audible voice declaring, 'You are my beloved Son, in whom I am well pleased'. Nor do I know of any other case in which the Holy Spirit has descended in visible form — as a dove — upon the candidate. His baptism was unique.

We have looked at just three instances from the first thirty years of the life of Jesus; but when we come to the three years of his public ministry, similar evidence comes tumbling in. Indeed, so overwhelming is the evidence of uniqueness that we are hard put to it to make sense of the events unless Jesus is none other than the Son of God from heaven, and different from every other human being to walk this earth.

Take the things that he *did*. There are some miracles of Jesus which modern doctors and psychiatrists have been able to duplicate. Many of them come in the category of psychosomatic disorders — cases where physical symptoms are caused by mental, emotional or moral disorders. When the inner disorder is treated, the outward symptoms disappear. So Jesus cures a paralysed man by forgiving his sins, removing the guilt that caused his paralysis. The modern psychiatrist will say that that can happen in his consulting room, too, and he may be right.

But no doctor or psychiatrist has stood in a boat and told a storm, 'Get down, stop jumping up at my disciples' (literally, Jesus said 'Be muzzled' as to a lively puppy, though I agree that 'Peace, be still!' sounds more beautiful). And no doctor or psychiatrist faced with a corpse of a man who had died four days ago would call him back to life by shouting his name — 'Lazarus!' It was because Jesus did things like this that people said, 'Only God can do the things he does ... What kind of man is this, whom even the winds and waves obey?'

Then, consider what he *was*. There was something about the character of Jesus that made ordinary, law-abiding people feel absolutely filthy and corrupt. 'Depart from me, for I am an evil man, oh Lord!' Peter pleaded after seeing one of his miracles. It happened time and time again. There was something about this man Jesus that was utterly good, and good in a way which people had never seen before. If one studies the three years of Christ's public ministry, it is impossible to find a point where one can say, 'There, see — he had a fault! I can feel closer to him now, because

he let himself down.' No one has been able to do
that. Jesus could go to his worst enemies and ask,
'Which of you can convict me of sin? Can you find
any fault in me?' None of us would dare put that
question even to our best friends, never mind our worst
enemies!

Consider, too, the things he *said*. 'I will judge the
world. One day you will all stand before me and I will
divide you into two groups, those bound for heaven,
and those bound for hell.' Or again: 'There is no way
to God except through me.'

A man who makes statements like those is either a
megalomaniac of the first degree . . . or else he is, as he
claimed to be, the Son of God. Indeed, one of the most
disturbing things about the ministry of Jesus was the
way in which he took to himself the sacred name of
God, 'I am' (in Anglicised Hebrew: 'Jehovah').
Sometimes — as in the Garden of Gethsemane — his
hearers were so terrified at his presumption that they
threw themselves to the ground, convinced that God
would strike him dead for his blasphemous arrogance.
But no divine lightning struck him down. In fact,
he capped it all at his trial. Asked directly to tell them
whether he was or was not the Son of God, he replied
equally directly, 'I am.'

Putting all of this together, it is surely ridiculous to
say that Jesus was 'just an ordinary human being', or
even a very unusual human being. There is something
here that simply cannot be fitted into any human
category: a truth that it took even his disciples a long
while to appreciate.

At the end of a holiday in the Holy Land I stood on
Mount Hermon — a hill 4,000 feet high ending in a
cliff-face from which bursts out a thirty-foot wide river,
born of the snow melting within the mountain. In that

cliff are niches, and within them used to stand carvings of ancient gods: Pan, who was supposed to have come to earth in human form, and Caesar, who claimed to be divine.

One day Jesus took his disciples to that very place and said to them: 'I've got a question for you. We've been together for two and a half years. You've lived with me, talked with me, shared my whole life with me. Now — who do people think I am?'

They replied that people regarded Jesus as a *reincarnation* of one or another of the great Jewish prophets, like Elijah.

Then Jesus put the first question to them again. 'But who do *you* say that I am?' And Peter, at that spot and at that moment in time, said, 'You are the Christ, the Son of the living God': not a superstar, not a reincarnated prophet, not a great human philosopher, but God *incarnate*.

What a moment! Jesus had waited throughout his ministry for that answer. Until it came he could not begin to fulfil the purpose of his coming: to go up to Jerusalem, to die and to rise again. No wonder he could now talk about 'building his Church' — now there is something to build on, the confession that its founder is the Christ, the Son of God. And the Church today, numbering millions, is made up of all those who share that confession of Peter.

A few days later Jesus took a few of his disciples up that very mountain, up above the snow line, and he was transfigured — transformed — before their eyes, dressed in clothes that were whiter than the glistening snow around them. For a moment they glimpsed eternity; its glory shone out from within Jesus, so that his very clothing was transparent to the light. They were seeing Jesus, their familiar friend, as he was in heaven before his coming to earth at Bethlehem, when he 'laid his glory by', and wrapped himself in human clay. That is why the traditional pictures of a fair-haired, blue-eyed man with a gleaming halo are very far from the truth. Jesus left his glory behind, apart from this moment of blinding revelation on the mountain.

Now let us turn to the last week of his life on earth, and sum up the facts briefly.

The time came when the enemies of Jesus wanted to accomplish his death. There was only one reason for this, only one charge in their minds, however much it was dressed up as treason for the sake of a Roman court. They were clear about his real offence: this man claimed to be God. For them this was the ultimate blasphemy — as indeed it would be, if it were not true — and the overwhelming motivation for their actions. Jesus died on the cross in the confidence that his God would reverse the human verdict, and that a higher court would prove his accusers wrong. In effect, he said, 'If I'm not the Son of God, then I will die and rot in my grave. But if I am the Son of God, in three days' time I will be back. God will raise me up.'

And so it happened. Three days after he died the rumours began to spread through Jerusalem that Jesus was alive again. Women went to the tomb to anoint a corpse and found none there. Others met him — in the cemetery-garden, on the road to Emmaus, in an upper room. The most cynical of Christ's followers, Thomas, having all but rejected the idea of the resurrection, within seven days became the first of the disciples to fall at the feet of the risen Christ and say, 'My Lord and my God!'

It is not unknown for people to fall down before a human being and call him God. Some people do it today. But let those self-styled 'gods' prove their divinity in the way Jesus did, by dying and being raised by the power of God.

As soon as one speaks of Jesus as 'God' the question is raised, 'Was he always God? And was he always man?' The answer to the first question is easy. No one can 'become' a God. By definition 'God' is self-existent, having no beginning and no end. So if Jesus is God at all, he has always been God.

But he has not always been man. I think that is one of the most amazing truths of Christianity. I have sometimes put it like this. Imagine a tank full of Siamese fighting fish. You notice that they are for ever fighting and killing each other. Now imagine that you were convinced that if only you became a fish and went into that tank with them you could do something about it — show them a better way. Would you do it? But more than that. Suppose you knew that if you did join them as a fish, their reaction would be to tear you to pieces and kill you. Would you do it then? And there is more than that to it. If by some miracle you survived and came back into the human world, you would come back as a fish and remain one for ever. Would you do it?

All analogies have their weaknesses, including that one. But it does at least bring home the incredible fact that Jesus is *still* a man. He did not just become man for thirty-three years and then 'revert' to divinity. His was no fleeting visit to humanity, 'slumming it' for a few years at our level. What he became, he cannot 'unbecome'.

And as a result, since Jesus became a man, and took that human nature back to heaven, human nature is right inside God. There is a man in heaven! There is a man to whom and through whom we can pray. There is a high priest 'who is touched with our infirmities', who understands and sympathises with our human dilemmas.

That the Son of God should consent not just to be a man among men, not just to face death at their hands, not just to suffer tears, loneliness and pain — but to remain a man for ever, to return to heaven as a man and to come back to this planet one day as a man: this is the Gospel.

But there is one more truth, a complementary truth, that is equally remarkable. Not only has human nature been taken right into God, but, through Jesus, the life of God can be placed within a man. In Jesus, in a way I cannot explain, all of God was concentrated in a single human being. As Charles Wesley put it, 'Our God contracted to a span, Incomprehensibly made man.' And now all the life of God that was in Jesus can be placed within me. That is also the Gospel.

6: Was it Suicide or Murder?

Gordon Bailey, an unorthodox evangelist and poet, was visiting homes on a housing estate. At one house a man opened the door and Gordon spoke to him.

'If you've got a few minutes to spare, I'd like to talk to you about Jesus.'

'I'm not interested in religion,' said the man.

'Who mentioned anything about religion?'

'Well, you did.'

'No, I didn't,' countered Gordon.

'Well anyway,' said the man firmly, 'You won't get me to church.'

'Who mentioned anything about church?'

'You did,' said the man, 'Didn't you?'

There was a moment's silence, and then Gordon suggested the best thing to do was start the conversation all over again. So they shut the door, Gordon rang the bell, and the man opened the door a second time.

'Now, listen very carefully,' said Gordon. 'If you've got a few minutes to spare I'd like to talk to you about Jesus.'

The man looked at him. 'Well, I'm still not interested.'

'What, not interested in the most famous man that ever lived?'

'Well, I wouldn't quite put it like that . . .'

'What do you know about him?' asked Gordon. 'Do you know how he died?'

'Yes. He died on a cross. Crucified.'

'Correct. But do you know that thousands of other people were crucified at about the same time?'

'No. I'd never thought about it.'

'So don't you think it's strange that out of all those people who were crucified, you've only heard of one?'

The man said, 'Come on in,' and they talked about Jesus for more than those 'few minutes'.

This chapter is about the cross: about why Jesus died, and why that one death is so important that it is remembered above everything else about him.

Here are a few thought-provoking facts about the death of Jesus.

Firstly, the cross, the symbol of our religion, was an instrument of torture and execution. Imagine walking into the temple of some unfamiliar religious sect and seeing as the centre-piece a scaffold, or a guillotine, or an electric chair. You would assume that that was a religion far from Christianity. And yet our symbol was the first-century Roman equivalent of those twentieth-century means of execution . . . and far more painful, ugly and degrading than any of them.

Secondly, Jesus lived as though his death were the most important thing he came to do. His ministry lasted at most three years, under the constant threat of assassination or judicial execution. He chose his time to die, but there can be no doubt that he regarded it as central to everything God desired of him.

Thirdly, the Gospels — our 'biographies' of Jesus — give as much as a third of their pages to describe the events of his death. Someone has said that they start like express trains — 'straight away' he did this, 'immediately' he went there — and then apply the brakes as his death draws near, until months give way to days and days to hours as his betrayal and death are related.

Fourthly, in the great statement of what the Church believes, the 'Apostles' Creed', there is not one word about the ministry of Jesus. We go straight from his birth to his crucifixion, with no mention of his wonderful teaching or his amazing miracles.

'. . . born of the virgin Mary, suffered under Pontius Pilate, was crucified, dead and buried . . .'

Fifthly, when Jesus gave his followers something to remember him by, it was a memorial of his *death*: broken bread, to represent his broken body, and wine poured out to represent his blood shed. When we wish to remember a loved one, we keep a photograph of them when they were fit and well and happy. But Jesus wants to be remembered as he died.

All of this adds up to one inescapable conclusion. In the thinking of Jesus, and in the practice of his followers ever since, his death is absolutely vital. To say this is not to endorse a morbid, depressing view of life, nor is it to ignore the life and teaching — and the resurrection — of Jesus. It is simply that his whole mission cannot be understood unless we give first place in it to that which he considered so important.

So as we look now at the cross, we are studying the central mystery and truth of our faith. Let us begin by dealing with views of the cross which, while they are not wrong in themselves, seem to me totally inadequate.

We are told, for instance, that Jesus died as an 'example' — an example of selfless love, or of self-sacrifice. Certainly the cross *is* an example of those things, but if that were all it would not justify its central position in our faith. When Jesus died he did something no mere human being could do. It was a unique action by a unique Person.

Then we are told that Jesus died as an 'exhibition'. I do not mean that in a cheap way. It is said that he died to exhibit to mankind how much God loves them and how far he will go to prove it.

Now again there is truth, and profound truth in that. On the cross Jesus revealed the love of God as a volcano erupting reveals the fire at the heart of the earth. God's burning love broke out into human sight at the cross. But that in itself would be a meaningless demonstration if it did not actually achieve anything in my life. When the New Testament talks of the cross it goes much further: 'Christ died for our sins according to the Scriptures' (1 Corinthians 15:3). The two key words there are 'sins' and 'scriptures', and unless we see the cross in the light of those two things we cannot possibly understand why Jesus died.

The Bible must be the clue to it all. God did not leave us to puzzle out the meaning — or rather, the meanings — of the cross for ourselves. It is all there in the Scriptures, and from the Scriptures I would like to draw out five 'meanings', basing them on the five letters of the word 'cross'.

In relation to the devil, the cross was a *Conquest*.

In relation to the world, the cross was a *Reconciliation*.

In relation to God, the cross was an *Offering*.

In relation to the law, the cross was a *Satisfaction*.

In relation to the sinner, the cross was a *Substitution*.

Let us now take those five statements and expand them.

1. In relation to the devil, it was a conquest

We saw in an earlier chapter that evil originally came from outside our world, through angelic beings who rebelled and then infected our planet with evil. Those evil beings still exist and are still at work. Satan is still the destroyer. Mankind ever since the Fall has been in the grip of evil. This 'cosmic' evil is beyond our powers to combat. It comes from beyond our world.

When Jesus set his face to go to the cross, it was this evil he was proposing to defeat. He took on Satan and all the powers of darkness, challenging them to do their worst in a final confrontation between God and his Adversary. Jesus went to his death in the belief that death would rob Satan of his power and make inevitable his final defeat.

Cornelius Ryan calls his book about D-Day *The Longest Day* — a phrase used by General Rommel, meaning that the war would be decided on the first day of the Allied invasion of Europe. If the invaders were beaten back, Hitler's empire would be safe. But if, on that 'longest day', the Allies were to establish a foothold on the Continent, then eventually victory would be theirs. Rommel was right. At the end of the 'longest day' the war was, in effect, over. There was a lot of bitter fighting still to be done and the mopping up was a long and painful business, but the eventual outcome was decided.

That is a good picture of the battle fought out on the cross. When Jesus died the war between good and evil was decided. There is still a lot of painful fighting to be done, and the mopping up is a slow and costly business, but the eventual outcome is assured. Satan's sting has been drawn, his power reduced. He is a defeated foe, and he knows it. The Christian who claims the victory of Christ on the cross can experience in practical daily terms the reality of that conquest.

Satan may have thought that the cross was his victory. It may have looked like that. But the resurrection proved that he was wrong. Indeed, after his resurrection Satan could no longer tempt Jesus, nor even speak to him.

After the resurrection, Jesus had nothing more to do with Satan. He was now a defeated foe.

2. In relation to the world, it is a reconciliation

'Reconciliation' means to bring together two alienated parties. Its most common use today is in matrimonial matters, where it describes the successful restoration of the relationship between an estranged husband and wife. If two people who were once together and subsequently became separated come together again, that is a 'reconciliation'.

In the relationship between God and man there was at first a perfect harmony, followed by an estrangement due to man's rebellion. Subsequently, there is a real antagonism in the human attitude towards God. This may be covered up by a professed belief in him, or even by church-going. But when fallen man is brought up against God's moral judgments, there is an antagonism, a rebellious attitude to God. And nothing can remove this antagonism but the cross.

Bishop Selwyn was a missionary to the Maoris of New Zealand in the early days of Queen Victoria. He once wrote home: 'I dwell in the midst of a people used to sin and uncontrolled from their youth. If I speak to them about murder, infanticide, adultery and cannibalism they laugh at me in the face and say these things are all right. But when I tell them that these and other things brought the Lord of Glory from his eternal home to this earth and to die, then they want to hear more, and by and by they acknowledge themselves as sinners.'

Tell the story of the cross to someone and the antagonism melts, their enmity towards God goes.

However, when one speaks of reconciliation it usually implies antagonism on both sides. Indeed, in many years of pastoral counselling I can only think of one estranged couple where there was a completely 'innocent' party — a man who came back from the war minus a leg and arm, deafened and blinded, and the day he arrived home his wife walked out of the house and never returned. In every other case there have clearly been faults on both sides.

But was this so in man's estrangement from God? Was there antagonism on God's side as well? No. God loves man and he's never hated him or been his enemy, no matter what man has done.

However, there *is* an antagonism on God's part — not an antagonism towards man himself, but towards his sin. He loves sinners but hates sin, and it is his antagonism to sin which is described as 'the wrath of God'. It is his righteous anger at the presence of sin in a world which he created perfect. His wrath is directed not at the victims of sin, but at sin itself, the great negative force of the universe. Like a condemned property, the earth is under judgment and ready for destruction. But some of its residents are not willing to leave it — even for vastly superior accommodation! — and they run the risk of being destroyed with the filthy, disease-ridden building whose days are numbered.

The Bible clearly teaches that the cross not only takes away man's antagonism towards God, but it also deals with God's antagonism towards sin. In Gethsemane, before the cross, Jesus prayed, 'Father, if it be possible, take away this cup from me.' Of the twenty times that the word 'cup' is used metaphorically in the Bible, on

all but three occasions it refers to the 'cup' of God's
wrath. It was that 'cup' which Jesus regarded with such
horror. It was as if, on the cross, Jesus drew into his
body all the wrath of God against the sin of the world.
He drank that 'cup' to the dregs. In that way, the cross
removes the antagonism in men towards God, and also
absorbs God's antagonism towards sin — and when
antagonism is taken away, reconciliation can be
achieved.

3. In relation to God, the cross is an offering
When Jesus died it was precisely three p.m. on the
fifteenth day of the month Nisan. That much we know
for sure. We cannot be certain of the year (it was
probably A.D. 29), but the day and hour have a very
great significance, because at three p.m. on the fifteenth
of Nisan, and on no other day, thousands of knives
slit the throats of thousands of lambs. At that moment,
the passover lambs were sacrificed as an offering to
God.

That kind of language means little to modern man,
because he is not used to the practice of sacrifice in
worship. For that you have to look at primitive socie-
ties, where animal, and even human, sacrifice has been
common.

For centuries before Jesus the Jews had slaughtered
innocent lambs as part of their worship, as an act of
'atonement' — to make amends, to pay compensation
for the sins they had committed. The idea behind it was
to offer to God a pure, unblemished life to make up
for the sinful life that God found in the worshipper.
And this was an idea to which God had given his
approval. He had said to the Jews, in effect, 'You must
make amends for the way you have lived, for the sins
and blemishes of your life. As it stands, I cannot accept

it. So take a lamb which is completely without spot or blemish, kill it and offer it to me. I shall accept its spotless, unblemished life as an atonement for your spoiled, blemished life.'

From the day when Jesus died there has been no need for lambs to be sacrificed. As John the Baptist, the cousin of Jesus, once said of him, 'That is the Lamb of God, who takes away the sin of the whole world.' Jesus provided the final and complete sacrifice which alone is able truly and totally to atone for our sin.

4. In relation to the law, the cross was a satisfaction

Laws undoubtedly solve some problems, but they also create one: what should be done to those who break them? It occurs in domestic life. When junior breaks a family rule, does the parent spank, or not spank? It occurs in our society. When a man commits a crime, do we try to reform him in a pleasant open prison, or would we do better to lock him up in a dark cell and feed him on bread and water and 'teach him a lesson'? All the while the dilemma is, do we punish or pardon? Do we show justice or mercy? We cannot do both, so whenever we have to deal with a wrongdoer — whether it is a naughty child or a hardened criminal — we have to decide which it shall be. God alone can avoid the dilemma, because God alone can be both just and merciful at the same time. He alone can punish *and* pardon.

How can he do this? In human experience the one can only be done at the expense of the other. The only situation in which both mercy and justice can be done is where an innocent person voluntarily accepts the punishment due to the guilty.

Imagine a court in which a helpless woman, abandoned by her husband, is found guilty and fined

seventy-five pounds or three months in prison. She has
no money, and she cannot bear the thought of parting
from her children, so she pleads with the judge for
mercy. But the judge cannot disregard the demands of
justice.

'You have broken the law,' he says, 'and the sentence
must stand.'

But then he takes out his cheque book and writes a
cheque for seventy-five pounds to pay the woman's
fine. He has, in one gesture, met the demands of justice
and mercy. The penalty has been paid, but the guilty
party walks out of court free. I have personally heard of
this situation occurring.

That is a picture of the way God solved the problem.
At the cross divine justice was satisfied; the price of sin
was paid in full. Yet the sinner, though guilty, is set
free ... provided he accepts the offering made on his
behalf.

5. In relation to the sinner, the cross is a substitution

That, in effect, is what we have just seen. Christ was
'substituted' for me, the guilty sinner. When a missionary preached about the cross to a group of Indians, one
of them cried out, 'Away from there, Jesus! That's not
your place, it's mine!' That is true. When Christ hung
on the cross, he hung there for me, as my 'substitute'.

There is a painting by Holman Hunt, the Pre-
Raphaelite artist who painted 'The Light of the World',
which is called 'The Scape-goat'. It is not well known,
because it is in a private art gallery in Manchester. He
regarded it as his major work — indeed, he spent two
years on the shores of the Dead Sea painting it.

It is a meticulously accurate painting of an animal,
a goat, which is dying under the weight of some
enormous, unseen burden. The title explains the picture:

this is the 'scape-goat' required on the Day of Atonement. The ritual is described in Leviticus chapter 16. On that day the Jewish people took a goat and 'transferred' their sins to it by laying their hands on its head and confessing them. Then the poor animal, laden (as it were) with the nation's sins, was driven out of Jerusalem into the wilderness to die.

Holman Hunt painted a goat, but in a way he was painting Christ; the very eyes are filled with sadness. He is the perfect 'scape-goat' to whom the Old Testament animal testified in advance.

So the cross is a complete and satisfactory way of dealing with man's sin without affronting the principle of justice. But its effectiveness requires faith on our part. When the sinner believes that Jesus died for him, in that moment his sins are forgiven and he has a place in heaven.

But that is not all. That is simply the beginning of a new kind of life — a life lived out every day in the light of the cross. The secret of that life is not just to say 'He died for me,' but to add, 'And I died with Him.' Christ is meant to be my substitute not only in death but in life. So that the life I now live is no longer mine, but the life of Christ, who died for me, and now lives in me. I died with him on the cross, and his risen life is mine as well.

So the cross is central to the whole business of becoming and being a Christian. That is why we preach 'Christ crucified' and glory in an instrument of death which has become the means of life.

7: Where In Heaven Did He Get To?

'On his robe and on his thigh he has a name inscribed, King of Kings and Lord of Lords.' So the book of Revelation describes the glory of Christ in heaven. But does the sentence convey to modern readers anything more than a mere shadow of what it meant to those who first heard it?

Take the word 'king'. The few 'kings' left in the western world are constitutional monarchs, figureheads who decorate ceremonial occasions and provide a device for maintaining parliamentary government between elections. Not long ago we watched on television the new King of Sweden being crowned just a few weeks after he had formally renounced the last vestiges of any real authority in the nation.

We cannot imagine the awe, the terrifying power which surrounded the absolute monarchs of the ancient world. It was not just that their word was law, even in matters of life and death. They were barely distinguishable from gods — indeed, in Rome and many other nations the absolute ruler was regarded as divine. It is only in the context of that kind of awe-inspiring power that we can get the full force of a title like 'King of Kings'.

It is much the same with the word 'lord' — our modern 'Lords' have much less real power than their counterparts in the House of Commons. In the ancient world the title has an interesting history. Beginning as the normal mode of address to a teacher by a pupil, it steadily acquired greater and greater dignity: a master over a servant, an owner over a slave, a ruler over a subject, and, eventually, a deity. So phrases have been discovered on parchment in Egypt dating back to ancient times invoking the deity: 'I prayed my lord Serapis for this' — 'lord' having become the title of a god.

In the Roman Empire the title became exclusive to the Emperor. 'Caesar is Lord'. Only two groups declined to give him this title. The Jews were given a legal dispensation on religious grounds. The Christians also refused to use it, but they were not given a legal dispensation and were thrown to the lions. For them there was only one Lord, Jesus, but it was a costly matter to stand up for this in Roman times. When calling Jesus 'Lord' might cost a believer his life, it is safe to say he would only do so if he really meant it.

But for us, the title has been devalued. With a general loss of respect for those in authority, and the disappearance of the concept of absolute power, it is harder for us to capture the thrill of this title. Perhaps Handel's music captures it for some of us: 'Kings of Kings and Lord of lords'. It is, in fact, a stupendous title: the ruler of the rulers, the governor of the governments, the chief power and authority in the universe.

How did Jesus acquire this title? By what right does he claim and receive such absolute power? There are three answers, and together they make up the 'three R's' of Christian worship. The title is his:

1. Because of his Resurrection.
2. Because of his Reign.
3. Because of his Return.

These are the three dimensions of the majesty of the Lord Jesus Christ.

1. Because of his Resurrection

The resurrection is the factor that sets Jesus apart from all the other kings and rulers. Not one of them has been able to overcome death. The world is littered with the tombs of royalty, including many who claimed to be, and were treated as divine.

All the pomp and power of yesterday finishes in the same way. As the poet puts it:

> *Death lays its icy hands on Kings . . .*
> *Sceptre and crown must tumble down,*
> *And in the dust be equal made*
> *With the poor crooked scythe and spade.*

No king, no lord, no ruler, no dictator or president has ever been able to conquer death. His body may survive for a time in a mausoleum or a glass-topped casket. His monuments may survive for centuries. But he is dead. Only Jesus defeated death. They died. He rose again.

Of course, many people have tried to reject or disprove the idea that Jesus rose from the dead. Some have suggested he was never really dead at all, but simply recovered from a coma and returned to his overjoyed disciples. Apparently this poor, crushed figure, three-quarters dead, having suffered a great loss of blood and much physical buffeting, not only recovered from his coma but also pushed aside the rock that sealed his tomb — a rock that normally required the combined strength of several fit, strong men to move it.

Others have suggested that the disciples were the

victims of hallucination — all of them, on all the different occasions when, together or individually, they saw the risen Jesus.

But most of the alternatives are even harder to believe than the resurrection itself. Indeed, the *evidence* in support of it is so strong that today, nearly two thousand years after the event, something like 700 million people believe that Jesus of Nazareth came back from the dead.

They *could* all be wrong, but it seems unlikely! The evidence of the empty tomb, of the folded grave-clothes, of the transformed disciples; of the change of the main day of worship from Saturday to Sunday; of the amazing establishment and growth of the infant Church in those early years after the crucifixion — all of these point to a powerful case for the resurrection.

Many of those who have set out to examine the evidence impartially — or even negatively, with a view to discrediting the Church's claims — have ended up convinced that the Jesus who died is now alive. The book *Who Moved the Stone?* is an example of just that kind of situation.

But it is not simply a question of the evidence for the resurrection. There is also the question of its *significance*. Why should Jesus come back from the dead? What is its meaning?

The answer is simple. At the crucifixion the world passed its verdict on Jesus. He was too bad to live. He was a blasphemer. He claimed to be God, and was not, and so must die. At the resurrection, on the other hand, God reversed the world's verdict on Jesus. He *is* the Son of God. He told the truth. Far from being too bad to live, he was too good to rot — 'my Holy One shall not see corruption,' God said.

But it is the *experience* of the resurrection that clinches

the issue for Christians. However much one studies the
evidence or examines the significance of the resurrection, it is only when the resurrection is experienced that
it becomes real. A friend of mine speaking in the open
air was asked by a heckler how he knew that Jesus rose
from the dead. 'Because I was talking to him this
morning,' he replied. That is what clinches it: the
personal experience of meeting the risen Lord — and he
is only truly 'Lord' to those who have met him.

2. Because of his Reign

The second reason why Jesus is King of Kings is
because of the reign he exercises now. And that reign
depends on what Christians call his 'ascension'. For
not only did Jesus rise from the dead, but he returned
to heaven, 'taken up' before the disciples' eyes ... the
first and last human being simply to 'step up' into
heaven, except perhaps Enoch or Elijah.

And in heaven he occupies the most honoured place,
the position described in the Bible as 'God's right hand'.
That place is the place of honour and glory, but it is
also the place of power and authority. Your 'right-hand
man' is the one who carries out your decisions. From
that honoured place Jesus executes his Father's will in
the universe. It is from there — 'seated at the right hand
of God' — that everything happens.

In the course of his very last conversation with his
disciples on earth Jesus said, 'All authority in heaven
and earth is given to me.' A man who talks like that is a
megalomaniac ... unless it is true. There were five
hundred people present when he said it, and no one
challenged his claim or described it as incredible. They
had come to know that he was stating no more than the
sober truth.

What a comfort that is! In all the events of this world

— in wars and confusion and revolution and change — Jesus is in authority. Everything that happens is ultimately controlled by him. And if at times it looks as though he has forgotten us, or has overlooked some area of gross injustice or scandal, all we are really seeing is the patience of God, waiting for us to repent rather than bring in the time of our judgment. But let us be sure of this: history has not got out of hand. It is not chaos. Jesus is in control.

However, it is not simply a matter of what Jesus is doing for us. Much more important is what he is doing for God. He is reigning as God's regent until all his enemies are beneath his feet.

Then all the kingdoms of the world will become the kingdom of our Lord Jesus Christ, and he will hand them back to the Father, so that 'God may be all in all'. When you read the daily papers you are reading about the Acts of Jesus Christ today: letting sin appear, showing up the devil in all his evil, and preparing, when man has done his worst, to step back on to the stage of history and bring righteousness and peace to this sad, sick world.

3. Because of his Return

That brings us to the third reason why Jesus is King of Kings — his return. Make no mistake, Jesus is coming back. Three hundred times the New Testament tells us that. How often must God say something before people believe it? The promise of Jesus on the night before he died was 'I shall come again'. A dying man tells the truth. That is the word of the dying Jesus, and he will keep it.

No one knows precisely when he will return. Imagine the reactions if people knew the date — some would panic, some would act foolishly, and some, I dare say, would reckon there was plenty of time to repent, and leave it until the last moment. It is far, far better that we do not know. Even Jesus while on earth did not know the exact day and time.

But we are given signs, so that those Christians who are alert and watching for them will not be taken unawares. And there is a feeling today in many parts of the world that those signs are being fulfilled, one after another.

Quite frankly, I do not expect Jesus to return immediately, because all the signs are not yet fulfilled, but at the present rate of change in the world who is to say when it might be? It could be in my life-time, or my children's. But whenever he comes, the vital thing is to be alert and ready, not to be taken unawares. 'Be sober, and watch.'

One of Hans Anderson's tales tells of an emperor who wanted to see how his people behaved in his absence. So he dressed as a beggar and visited the city. They threw him out! A few days later, when he came in triumph in his golden carriage, everybody bowed low as it passed; but when they looked into the carriage to see the emperor, they were astonished to see the face of the beggar they had treated so badly.

People have rejected Jesus for two thousand years. They have dismissed him as a 'mere man', with no claim on their allegiance. But like the citizens in the story, they will see that the 'beggar' is in fact the 'emperor', the man of Galilee is the King of Kings. The sign of his first coming was a single star in the eastern sky, but the sign of his second coming will be like lightning from the east to the west, filling the whole sky. At that moment every knee will bow, and every tongue — for joy, or in fear — will confess him Lord of all.

What will Christ do when he returns? Three things. Firstly, he will openly *defeat* the forces of evil that have enslaved this planet so long. I believe there will be a terrible confrontation between good and evil in the last days of history. The evil plans of Satan will climax in the reign of a world ruler (described in the Bible as the 'Antichrist') who will try to usurp the very place of Christ himself. It is from that evil that Jesus will come to liberate us — to take Satan, bind him and cast him out for ever.

It is no human foe that Christ will face, for it is not human evil that causes our enslavement, Satan is the father of wars, hatred and suffering, and only his defeat can bring them to an end.

Then, secondly, Christ is coming to *divide* the human race in two, just as once he divided history into B.C. and A.D. The dividing line may run through families, and church congregations, too. He is going to divide the sheep from the goats, the wheat from the tares, the wise virgins from the foolish ones. 'From thence he will come to judge the quick and the dead.'

Thirdly, he is coming to *deliver* his own people, those who love him. I believe the Church is going to go through more and more suffering. It is going to get tougher to stand as a Christian, as Satan builds up for his last desperate bid to keep the kingdoms of this world. We are warned in the Bible that the blood of the saints is going to flow like rivers until the souls of those martyred cry out beneath the altar for vengeance.

And then Christ will come — to avenge his saints, to reverse the apparent victory of evil and to overthrow Satan. When all seems most lost, when the outlook is darkest — that is the moment of the triumph of Christ, when men will see that he truly is 'Lord of all'.

The nearest the early Christians came to a creed was

a simple three-word confession: 'Jesus is Lord'. That is the heart of discipleship, and the heart of what we believe. Life will only work one way, and that is when Jesus is Lord. Paul the headstrong, ambitious young man came to the point where he called himself a slave of the Lord Jesus. It was the moment of victory. When your Christian life goes wrong, and problems and difficulties arise, invariably the cause is very simple. At some point Jesus is not Lord.

Not only the individual Christian life, but the life of the Church, too, will only work when Jesus is Lord. Churches get into moral trouble, or are divided and in dispute, when Jesus is not Lord in the life of his people. It is also true in the life of the world. Politicians, economists, statesmen and negotiators try to put things right, but the world will only work one way — when Jesus is Lord. There can be no real peace until the Prince of peace is acknowledged.

Finally, to those who are searching for some meaning, for some integrating point in life — including those whose lives, though young, are already in chaos morally, intellectually or emotionally: life will become purposeful, meaningful and integrated when Jesus is Lord.

That is what we believe. As the old prayer puts it, 'King of Kings, Lord of lords, the only ruler of princes' — Jesus is Lord!

8: S.O.S.

Three coal-miners are trapped by a rock-fall several thousand feet below the surface. There may be poisonous gas; there may be an explosion. At the surface every available man, and every obtainable mechanical device, is pressed into service. Television cameras, arc lights, the anxious relatives at the pit-heads — we have all seen it on our screens. And then, after many anxious hours, the miners are brought up alive. They have been *saved*.

Or there is the familiar holiday incident. A swimmer gets into difficulties several hundred yards from the beach. His struggles are noticed by an alert life-guard, who dashes out into the surf and swims powerfully to the spot where he last saw the drowning man. By now he has stopped struggling. He is lying just below the surface, motionless. The life-guard pulls him to the shore, and begins mouth to mouth resuscitation. Half an hour later the first breath of life animates the man's chest. He is alive. He has been *saved*.

In situations such as those it is natural to use the word 'saved'. Someone was in peril, at the point of death. And by the efforts of a third party they were rescued from their plight . . . saved. Yet when we use the same verb in talking of a religious experience, or ask 'Are you saved?' it seems in some way artificial. After all, these pleasant, respectable, law-abiding people in the pews — where is the need for them to be 'saved'? The word seems too stark, too extreme.

And so does the word 'salvation', which has the same root with such words as safe, saved and salvage. It is a very 'big' word, with many shades of meaning, and it is at the very heart of what we believe. So we are going to examine seven factors involved in 'salvation', in 'being saved'.

1. Salvation is from sin.
2. Salvation is after repentance.
3. Salvation is by grace.
4. Salvation is through faith.
5. Salvation is with assurance.
6. Salvation is to holiness.
7. Salvation is for eternity.

1. Salvation is from sin

We have all got troubles. Indeed, sometimes one begins to think there is nothing but trouble in the world. In the last few years I have been more aware of people coming with their problems and troubles than ever before in my ministry. Loneliness, fear, boredom, ignorance, poverty — troubles abound; but what is *the* trouble? What is the cause of it all?

As we saw in an earlier chapter, the answer is sin. That is God's explanation of all our troubles. If you are coming to God to get all the other troubles sorted out, but do not bring him this one, you are unlikely to find a real solution. We present our problems, but God's diagnosis is that the root problem, the heart of the disease, is sin.

Imagine a patient who visits his doctor, who is also his friend, to tell him that he is lonely and feeling a bit down. But as they chat, the doctor notices certain symptoms — in the patient's eyes, perhaps, or in a spasm of his limbs, or the colour of his lips — and comes to the conclusion that he may be suffering from a very serious illness indeed. He tries to talk about these symptoms, to ask questions about the patient — general health, and particular questions relating to this disease. But his visitor will not have it. He prattles on about how lonely and bored he is, until the doctor bluntly interrupts and says, 'Do you mind if I tell you something? I believe you are suffering from a very dangerous disease, far more serious than your boredom and isolation. If you don't let me examine you and get treatment started, I'm afraid it won't be long before your other little troubles will stop bothering you.'

But suppose his patient will have none of it. 'No, no,' he may say, 'I can't accept that. I don't believe I'm that ill. It's just that I'm bored and lonely.'

When we come to God with our day-to-day troubles and problems, I believe he wants to deal first with the root of *all* our troubles, sin. That is the deadly disease, of which all our other problems are merely the symptoms. Sin numbs our 'spiritual nerves' so that we do not feel acutely the evil of sin, nor the presence of God all around. We become spiritually insensitive.

That is why sin is such a deadly disease. It is not just a question of wrong things we *do* — the breaking of God's laws. It goes much deeper. It is what we *are*, inherited from our parents and their parents before them ... a congenital disease. And it is a progressive disease, too, steadily eroding our God-given faculties, blinding us to truth and goodness, until finally we are spiritually dead, no longer able to relate or respond to God at all, or even to goodness. It is from that fate, which Jesus describes as 'hell', that we need saving.

2. Salvation is after repentance

What is 'repentance'? Does it mean feeling sorry —

desperately sorry, perhaps — for what we have done? That is remorse, and it is a commendable feeling, but it is not repentance. Most of us are sorry about the consequences of our sin: the punishment, the damaged relationships, the recriminations and scandal. Repentance, as the schoolboy said, is being sorry enough to stop. Martin Luther put it slightly more theologically: 'the truest repentance is to do it no more'. A well-known evangelist used to make his appeal at the end of a meeting in these terms: 'Don't come out to the front to accept the Saviour unless you're prepared to leave your sins on your seat!'

That is what repentance is all about: being willing to let our sins go. It shows we really want to be saved, and know what it is from which we are being saved. What is quite impossible is to have our sins *and* have salvation. The two are mutually exclusive.

3. Salvation is by grace

A man in East Anglia once said, 'It took me forty-three years to discover three things. Firstly, that I could do nothing to save myself. Secondly, that God did not require me to do anything. Thirdly, that Christ had done it all.'

By nature human beings are suspicious of anything that is offered free of charge. A story is told about a wealthy man who stood on the Tyne Bridge in my home town, Newcastle, trying to give away pound notes. He found hardly any takers. Most people avoided him, or moved away. They could not believe that there was no trick in it.

It may be that we are too proud to accept 'charity', or afraid of hidden 'strings', but this suspicion and distrust is a terrible barrier. Old people refuse to seek financial help from the social services. Others in all kinds of need are reluctant to ask for what is freely offered, often because of pride: 'I've always stood on my own feet, and I'm not going begging now.'

That is one reason why it is so hard for people to accept God's grace, for 'grace' means two simple things: bad deeds are no hindrance, and good deeds are no help when you come to God for salvation.

It does not matter what dreadful things you may have done in the past. They cannot put you beyond redemption. And it does not matter what good deeds you may have done in the past either. They cannot save you. Indeed, they may be a hindrance, if you come to God not empty-handed (as he requires) but with one hand full of your own goodness. It takes both hands empty to receive grace. As Toplady's hymn puts it:

> Nothing in my hand I bring,
> Simply to thy cross I cling.

Salvation is 'by grace'. It may take us a whole lifetime of struggling before we realise that there is no salvation that way, and learn that there is nothing a man can do to save himself. God requires nothing of us; Christ has done it all.

4. Salvation is through faith

Prepositions can be crucial, and they are in discussing salvation. It is *by* grace, *through* faith. Faith is only the link; grace provides the power.

So — what *is* faith? The first thing to establish is that it is not a matter of feeling. Martin Luther once said, 'I do not feel that my sins are forgiven, but I know they are because God has said so in his Word.' Faith is not feeling, although wonderful feelings may follow faith in Christ. In a sense, when the Holy Spirit takes hold of a person he releases his feelings in a new way, freeing him from inhibitions that have been bottled up before, and prevented him from experiencing love, joy and peace. But it is not the feeling that is the faith; the faith creates the feeling.

Nor is faith primarily a matter of thought. Thought is involved of course. There is a certain minimum intellectual content necessary for faith: the deity of Jesus, for instance, his death and his resurrection. But if you recite the Creed and say 'I believe all of that with my mind' you are 'believing' no more than the demons ... and they do a bit more, the Bible tells us: the thought of it makes them 'tremble'.

So, what *is* faith? Faith is to take those truths and apply them personally: to say, 'Jesus died for *me* — rose for *me* — and is coming back for *me*.' The devils cannot share that belief, that kind of faith.

Faith is, in a sense, an act of trust in which the believer takes his life and puts it into the hands of Christ. It is a daily thing — committing myself into the hands of another. In ordinary life we do it all the time — every time we board an aeroplane or a bus, every time we put ourselves into the hands of a surgeon. Faith is just that: putting my ruined life into the hands of Jesus and giving him responsibility from that point on.

5. Salvation is with assurance

It is God's will that you should know you are his. When people ask 'Are you saved?' he does not expect his children to answer, 'I hope so', 'I'm trying' or 'I'd like to think I am.' He wants us to be sure of it, not with arrogance but with faith; not sure of ourselves, but sure of him and his promises.

This assurance comes through his word of promise at first, but it also, and perhaps more profoundly, comes from our consciences, as they begin to assure us that at last we are free of this destructive thing called sin, that there is a change in our manner of life, and that we are children of God. Above all God wants to plant in our hearts the fullness of the Holy Spirit. It is by this gift that his children can call him 'Father'. After all, it is the birthright of children, and he intends it for us.

There are people who believe in God and trust in Christ. Through faith they have received the grace of salvation. But they still lack assurance. They worry and fret about their standing before God, and so their testimony is weakened. For such people the great need is to ask God to take them one step further, to pour his Holy Spirit into their hearts to bear witness to the fact that they are children of God, bound for heaven.

6. Salvation is to holiness
Salvation is not only 'from' sin, but 'to' holiness. In other words, it is not simply a negative exercise. The Bible talks about being 'saved *to* the uttermost', but very often preachers interpret that as though it meant '*from* the guttermost'. We are saved for a purpose, a destiny: and that destiny is holiness.

It is a sobering thought that we are as holy as we want to be, no more and no less. I do not believe that there is a 'package deal' in holiness, to be received once and for all, perhaps at a convention, and then forgotten. Holiness is a moment by moment relationship with God, not a static thing. Nevertheless, I know that there are occasions when one has been filled with the Spirit and holiness no longer seems an unattainable, distant ideal, but a present reality. At such times one has known that it is possible not to sin; indeed, it would be impossible, so real and intense is the presence of God. It is God's will that that should become our normal, day-by-day experience.

T–D

Holiness is not the same as happiness. In fact, sometimes unhappy experiences can lead us into holiness. Sometimes he chastises us to lead us into holiness. Sickness, pain, disappointment may do for us what prosperity and ease can never achieve, and help to make us holy.

7. Salvation is for eternity

I heard Professor Christian Barnard, the pioneer of heart-transplant surgery, talking on the radio about his successes. He remarked, with obvious satisfaction, that some of his patients lived for a further eighteen months, and one had even survived for three years. He was thrilled to have saved a person's life for eighteen months or three years. But when God saves he saves for eternity: totally, and permanently. And that must include holiness: 'You shall be perfect, as my Father in heaven is perfect.' God has never done anything by halves. Salvation is for ever, or it is not salvation at all.

There are two final comments I should like to make about salvation. The first is that it is a process, not a crisis. Salvation is continuous, and the process is not yet complete in any of us. If I am asked, 'Are you saved?' the true answer is, 'I am being saved' — I am in the process of salvation. The important question is, where am I in this process? And am I making progress, or standing still?

The other comment is that salvation, although it is a process, is not mechanical. It is not like an assembly-line. Salvation is personal because it is a Person. It involves recognition of sin, repentance, grace, faith, assurance, holiness, and it lasts for ever. But it all centres in a Person, and without him it is nothing. Salvation, in one word, is Jesus.

9: Got a Conversion Complex?

Throughout the nineteen-seventies, most cities and towns in Britain became familiar with the idea of conversion. My wife and I, for example, were converted three years ago. This is how it happened.

For some time our town had been covered with posters asking, 'Have you been converted yet?' Then a leaflet was pushed through the door. It spoke about a radical and important change which would deeply affect our way of life, and warned of dangers if we were not converted. Subsequently a man called to talk it over with us, and a few days later we were converted. As he had promised, it made a lasting difference. Ever since, we have cooked by natural gas.

As it happens, the gas industry has been using the word 'conversion' correctly, and when Christians use the word in its spiritual sense, the process is almost identical. Conversion (to natural gas, or to Christ) leaves the exterior as it was — the same cooker, the same fires; the same long nose, fair hair and so on. But in both cases there is a new inside. Something is taken away and discarded, and there is a radical replacement — something essential is changed. And in both cases there is subsequently a new power. Natural gas burns with greater heat than manufactured gas, and in the spiritual realm there is little doubt that conversion leads to an altogether 'warmer' kind of religion.

But what exactly *is* conversion — religious conversion that is? Its most common usage is to describe a person who changes from one religion to another (Muslim to Christian, for instance) or even from one denomination to another (particularly Roman Catholic to Protestant, or vice versa). So one might be tempted to think that if one remained in one denomination all one's life there was no need at all for conversion.

But according to the words of Jesus, conversion is absolutely vital for everybody. 'Unless you are converted ... you will not see the Kingdom of heaven.' So obviously it is an important process to understand. We shall be considering it from two angles or perspectives, the divine — what God does; and the human — what man does.

The divine aspect of conversion

Although many people would say that they were converted by Billy Graham, that is a claim the evangelist himself always rejects. 'Billy Graham never converted anyone,' he says.' Only God can.'

There is certainly an element of truth in this. I could not convert my boiler to natural gas. It was simply beyond me. And converting myself in a spiritual sense is even further beyond me. Only those who have tried to convert themselves know how utterly impossible it is. After all, to satisfy God's standards we need to be saints: absolutely perfect, absolutely holy. Converting oneself to *that* standard sounds difficult, and in practice proves impossible.

Martin Luther tried desperately to convert himself, submitting his body to awful indignities, denying himself even food and rest in a sincere and determined attempt to satisfy God's standards. He failed miserably.

What he, and many others down the centuries, eventually found was that it was not a new start in life they needed, but a new life to start with. After all, it takes a Creator to make new life. And that is the miracle which Jesus described very vividly as being 'born all over again'. It is God's answer to the kind of prayer King David prayed after he had sinned and failed God so badly: 'Create in me a clean heart, O God, and renew a right spirit within me.' There is the double aspect of conversion: a new 'inside' in an old 'outside' . . . and a new source of power.

And without that change, without conversion, according to the words of Jesus, we shall never see the kingdom of God. We need to be converted, he said, 'and become like little children'. We need, in other words, to start life all over again, but this time with a new power and a new principle within us.

It was this that Nicodemus had to learn. This gifted Jewish leader came to Jesus secretly, by night, to enquire about his teaching, and was told, quite abruptly, 'You must be born again'. It would never be enough for the respectable and devout Nicodemus simply to follow a new code of doctrine or ethics. He, like all the rest of us, needed a new nature. He needed to be converted.

The human aspect of conversion

So how does conversion come about? If it is a divine act, do we simply wait for it to strike, like lightning from heaven? Or is it, as some people suggest, just a matter of temperament? Are some of us by temperament 'once born' people, and some 'twice born'? Is there a human element in the process?

Indeed there is. In fact, in one respect it is *not* true to say that 'only God' can convert someone. The New Testament talks of *men* 'converting' sinners from the error of their ways. It even talks of sinners converting *themselves*. Jesus told Peter that when he had converted himself (that is the literal translation) he should strengthen his brethren. Surprisingly, not once is the Lord the subject of the verb 'convert'!

The human side of conversion is rather more complex than one might imagine. There are at least five elements in it.

1. Repentance from sin

This aspect of conversion, and the next one, were dealt with in the previous chapter, so perhaps here all one need say is that turning *to* God (which is what conversion is) assumes a turning *from* sin. We turn away from the old life, with all that that involves, and turn to the new life that Christ gives.

There is no half-way in this process. It involves a willingness to be rid of every evil thing, however dear it is to us, and even some neutral things (like certain relationships, hobbies or pursuits) which while harmless in themselves have got between us and God. In this latter area there are no hard and fast rules, beyond this simple test: is this thing so integrally a part of my old life that I cannot keep it and still turn completely to God? Repentance is simply the willingness to turn, without condition.

2. Faith towards Jesus

This, as we have already seen, is a total trust in Christ's competence to do what he has promised. In his life, death and resurrection, he has totally mastered evil. 'Faith' means believing that he can repeat that mastery in me, create in me a clean heart and renew a right spirit within me.

3. *Baptism in water*

Baptism is part of the process of conversion, although it is often, but wrongly, regarded as separate from it. It is not something extra, added later, but part of the single process of Christian initiation.

If baptism and conversion are two separate and distinct things, there are a number of statements in the New Testament that become totally inexplicable:

'He who believes and is baptised will be saved' (Mark 16: 14).

'Unless one is born of water and the Spirit, he cannot enter the Kingdom of heaven' (John 3: 5).

'Repent and be baptised . . . for the forgiveness of your sins' (Acts 2: 38).

'Rise and be baptised, washing away your sins' (Acts 22: 16).

'Christ loved the Church . . . having cleansed her by the washing of water with the word' (Ephesians 6: 25f).

'God our Saviour . . . saved us . . . by the washing of regeneration and renewal in the Holy Spirit' (Titus 3: 4f).

'Baptism . . . now saves you' (1 Peter 3: 21).

These are strong statements and they make high claims for baptism. Indeed, taken literally they seem to imply almost a magical power to this rite, as though to baptise someone is to make him a Christian. However, there is no need to take so obviously extreme and misleading a view. All of the 'difficulties' in these verses disappear when baptism is seen as one element in conversion. Once we get rid of the idea that we are first converted and then baptised, we can see how the two words can correctly be used to describe the same event. Baptism is part (indeed, the most obvious and visible part) of conversion, and is therefore part of Christian initiation.

In passing, if someone is converted but not baptised, we may correctly see the process of conversion as incomplete. Baptism, in that case, completes their conversion.

Basically, baptism is two things, a burial and a bath. It is the disposal of the old life, 'buried with Christ in baptism', and the starting clean with the new one, coming up out of the water into the new, risen life. Nothing could possibly represent more vividly than that what conversion is all about.

4. Filling with Holy Spirit

Now we turn to the element of power in conversion. The principle involved here is rather similar to that in baptism, and the most common error about it is the same one — that conversion and 'being filled with Spirit' are two entirely separate things. Indeed, like many young Christians, I believed for many years that to be filled with Spirit was a remote target set for the believer, only to be achieved — if at all — after years of emptying my life of self and sin. It came as quite a shock to discover that the Bible taught a rather different view: being filled with Spirit, like baptism, is meant to be part of the process of conversion.

If we take the references to being filled with Holy Spirit in the Acts of the Apostles, we shall find a consistent pattern emerges. In Acts 2, on the day of Pentecost, it was not only the apostles who were filled with Spirit. It is true that they 'received' Holy Spirit, as the summit experience of their discipleship. They had spent the best part of three years with Jesus, absorbing his teaching and observing his miracles, so perhaps for them it may have seemed a kind of 'target' that was achieved on the day of Pentecost. But on that same day Peter, being himself now filled with Spirit, promised precisely the same experience to *all* those who heard his words, believed them and were baptised. 'The promise is to you, and to your children, and to as many as the Lord your God shall call . . .' The Holy Spirit's power was offered as *part of conversion*, not a target to be reached at some remote, later date.

Then in Acts 8 we read of Philip's mission to Samaria, when great crowds believed and were baptised. But they did not 'receive' Holy Spirit. Far from being regarded as a normal or acceptable situation, this deficiency was treated as a matter of extreme urgency. Peter and John went down to Samaria to lay their hands on these new believers so that they, too, should be filled with Holy Spirit. Clearly until that happened they were regarded as only partly converted.

When Saul of Tarsus was converted (Acts 9: 17), he received Holy Spirit within the context of his conversion experience. The Roman centurion Cornelius and his friends (Acts 10: 44) received Holy Spirit before they were baptised, so that Peter could ask, 'Who can forbid baptism to these Gentiles, seeing they have had the same experience as we have?' In this case, it was baptism that 'completed' the conversion.

Then in Acts 19 we have the remarkable case of the disciples at Ephesus. Of the five elements of conversion that I suggested earlier, these disciples had experienced only one — repentance through the ministry of John the Baptist. They had not fully believed in Jesus, they had not had Christian baptism, they had not been filled with Spirit and they had not become members of a church. Paul led them to belief in the One to whom John the Baptist pointed, he baptised them in the name of the Lord Jesus, and then he laid his hands on them and they received Holy Spirit, spoke in tongues and prophesied. Notice that there were different ways in which this experience showed, but that a person who had been filled up usually overflowed through the mouth!

There is the full spectrum of conversion, and until all these elements are present no one can be described as truly converted. Certainly receiving power through the gift of Holy Spirit is a vital part of being converted to Christ. He baptises in Spirit, he fills with Spirit, he pours out Spirit. The neglect of this element in conversion may account for the presence of so many ineffective Christians in the churches. They have not received 'power'.

5. Membership of a church

The fifth element in conversion may be for some readers the most controversial of all — membership of a church. There are some 'freelance' Christians who wander from church to church, familiar with many of them, genuinely committed to none of them. At the other extreme there are people who argue that it is possible (and even preferable) to believe in Christ without 'going to church'. Both attitudes reveal a misunderstanding of God's purpose in saving men and women.

His aim, from the very beginning, was to make a body — not many bodies — to glorify him for ever; and to deliver us from individualism (which is a form of self-centredness) into a community. This 'body' is not simply a concept. It expresses itself on earth in local churches. Paul, writing to 'the church of God which is in Corinth', assured them, 'You *are* the body of Christ (N.B. Not part of it) and individually members of it.' The New Testament knows nothing of Christians who are, or at any rate remain, unrepentant, unbaptised, unfilled ... or *unchurched*. It simply assumes that all those who believe in Christ are integrated into the local church under local leaders.

On the day of Pentecost the conversion of three thousand people was described in the New Testament in these words: 'Those who received the word were baptised, and there were added that day about 3,000 souls.' But why *added*? Added to what? The answer has to be, added to the church in Jerusalem. The next sentences relate the sequel, as these new church members 'devoted themselves to the apostles' teaching and fellowship, to the breaking of bread and the prayers'. At once, as part of their conversion, they were church members and began to engage in church activities.

Repentance and faith are the basics of conversion, but they would only be adequate to save us if we were dying! If conversion means embarking on a new *life*, then the other three elements are not optional extras but absolute essentials. 'We are *baptised* in one *Spirit* into one *body*', Paul told the Corinthians. There is the total picture of Christian initiation in one sentence.

To leave the body, the church, out of that is to omit the corporate aspect and to imply that conversion is a highly individual, private matter. In fact, we are converted to the church at the same time as we are converted to Christ. We cannot separate the Head from the body.

And that body is not a vague, disorganised shambles. Under its Head, Christ, it is a structured, disciplined body, with leaders appointed and authorised by Christ himself. Christians are to 'obey your leaders and submit to them' (Hebrews 13: 17).

So the important question is not, 'Have you been converted?' but 'Have you been *fully* converted?' Are all of these five elements present in your conversion? They belong together — and what God has joined together let no man put asunder! None is an optional extra, nor is any of them intended to be a later, 'second blessing'. Many troubles in the Christian life, many unnecessary doubts and disappointments, are traceable to an attitude which sees one or other of them as separate from the rest, or sufficient on its own. It is the total experience, the whole experience, which alone can accurately be called conversion.

10: That's the Spirit!

I began preaching about thirty years ago and I celebrated twenty-five years of ministry in 1975. During those years there have been many, many changes in church life, the great majority of them for the better. But the greatest change of all, and the one that makes me more optimistic and more excited about the prospects now than ever before in my ministry, is that the Church has again begun to recognise that there are *three* Persons in the Godhead, not two.

Of course I know that the Church has always officially held that there are three Persons in the Godhead, Father, Son and Holy Spirit. But in practice there were only two. The Holy Spirit had become the 'displaced person' of the Trinity. We believed that there *was* a Holy Spirit; we did not really believe *in* Him. This was evident in our vocabulary, in our worship and prayers, in our hymns and in our preaching. Like other ministers, I would manage a sermon on the Holy Spirit at Whitsun, in the assurance that I should not be expected to produce another one until his next anniversary. In practice, it has been said, Roman Catholics believed in the Father, the Son and the Holy Virgin, and Protestants in the Father, the Son and the Holy Bible. Certainly the Holy Spirit, as a living, dynamic Person, hardly featured prominently in the life of either church.

Now that has changed. Indeed, the situation has almost entirely reversed. Our relationship to the Holy

Spirit has become conscious, rather than unconscious; direct, rather than indirect; dynamic rather than doctrinal, and a matter of intuition rather than inference. He is constantly referred to, discussed and debated, and there is a steady stream of books about him.

It was alleged that if the Church turned its attention to the Holy Spirit, Jesus Christ would be neglected. In the event, this has not happened. Indeed, this period of interest in the Holy Spirit has also seen a marked growth of interest in Jesus, not only in the Church, but outside as well. Not surprisingly, we are finding that there is no 'competition' within the Trinity. To magnify one member is to magnify the Godhead.

However, problems have arisen over this new emphasis on the Holy Spirit. There have been disturbances, and even divisions, within the Church. Many of these have arisen through misunderstandings and misconceptions about the Holy Spirit, which themselves flow from a strange distrust of teaching about his Person and ministry.

This distrust is shared by two quite different sets of people. Those who are afraid and suspicious of anything new in the Church — and especially anything involving emotion or disturbance — need to be taught about the Holy Spirit, but resist because they are afraid of being drawn into unwelcome experiences.

Those who welcome the experiences, however, also resist teaching, because they fear that it will come between them and their experiences. In the event, without teaching they may easily lapse into fanaticism, just as the others may drift into an inflexible and cold conservatism.

But God wants people with warm hearts *and* warm heads, people who feel *and* think, who experience *and* understand. He is not a God of disorder and confusion.

So in this chapter I want to look at the doctrinal aspects of the Holy Spirit — who he is, and what he does. Then in the following chapter we shall look at the other aspects of the subject, and especially his role in the life of the believers.

1. Who He Is

a. His personality

The story is told of a little girl who watched awe-struck as the vicar walked into church dressed in a gleaming white surplice. 'Is that the Holy Ghost?' she whispered to her mother.

As it happens, she was two-thirds right. She expected the Holy Spirit to be a *person*: and she expected to see that person in church. Her error was simple: the vicar was not the Holy Spirit.

But how many church people would get those other two points right? Many speak of the Holy Spirit as though he were a 'thing', and 'it', a floating force or atmosphere. And few would seriously expect to meet him in church.

In fact, his title — 'the Holy Spirit' — tells us precisely what we need to know about who he is. For instance, the definite article 'the' distinguishes him from an impersonal force or influence. He is not *a* spirit of good-will, charity or kindness. He is *the* Spirit of God. Everything we read about him in the Bible speaks of personality. All the things done by him are personal: he speaks, searches, cries out, prays, teaches, forbids. And all the things done to him are things that can only be done to a person, not to a thing: we can grieve him, lie to him, resist him, blaspheme him. All of these verbs speak of personality.

But the clearest teaching about the personality of

the Holy Spirit is in our Lord's teaching on the night before he died, recorded in John's Gospel chapters fourteen to sixteen. Here he explains that though he, Jesus, is going away, his followers will not be orphaned. Someone else was being sent to replace him, someone like him, who would not only do all he had done for them but even more. And that 'someone else' was the Holy Spirit.

When Jesus said that 'another' would come, the Greek word used is the one that means 'similar', rather than an alternative available word which means 'another but different'. The Holy Spirit is a Person, like Jesus. When Jesus went away, he sent another Person to replace him and dwell in the believer.

I am sorry that a word like 'Comforter' ever got into any translation of the Bible as a title of the Holy Spirit. Comfort is indeed what many seek from religion, but comfort (in the simple sense) is the last thing we should expect from the Holy Spirit. He is a moving Spirit, a disturber, a changer of people and circumstances.

To say that he is a 'Power' is to under-state the case. Electricity is a 'power', and when you have it installed in your house, the power can be used. But all the while you use the power, it is under your control. Indeed, you can manipulate it in any way you desire.

But when the Holy Spirit is 'installed' in your life, although it is true there is a new source of power, it is not under your control, like electricity. He cannot be manipulated or switched on and off. You can no more direct him than you can tell the wind where to go!

His presence is more like that of a guest in the house. He affects our relationships. His views and attitudes have to be taken into account when making family decisions. He changes people and he changes situations, *simply because he is a Person himself*.

b. His purity

There are many unholy 'spirits' abroad in the world today, and it is tragically possible for people to be taken over by them. Alcohol is one such. 'Don't be drunk with wine ... but be filled with the Spirit,' Paul wrote to the Ephesians. In other words, reject an unholy spirit, and receive the Holy Spirit. Indeed, there is a sort of similarity between the two cases, because in both cases the person involved is 'taken over' by the spirit. It is the spirit who speaks (think of the saying about 'the wine talking') and controls a willing slave. In fact, on the day of Pentecost the first reaction of the bystanders was to assume that the disciples were intoxicated with wine. But the similarity is superficial. The motivating power is different — the difference between a holy and an unholy spirit.

Hysteria is another unholy spirit. People are 'worked up' to such a pitch that they become incapable of reason and respond irrationally. The films of Hitler's pre-war rallies at Munich and elsewhere are frightening in their revelation of the way an orator can first drive his audience into hysteria, and then control their responses like a puppet-master.

Similarly, the sight on television of young girls weeping or screaming hysterically at the distant vision of their favourite pop star is very disturbing. They, too, have surrendered their reason.

Mania is another unholy spirit, and I certainly include religious mania in that. Festus accused Paul of being a religious maniac (Acts 26: 24), but of course the apostle was nothing of the kind.

Mania is irrational. It takes over a person, until they have no control over their responses. The spirit of mania (derangement, madness) is unholy. The Spirit of God is sanity, wholeness and light.

Perhaps the deadliest of all the unholy spirits is the spirit of *possession*, because that is directly demonic. More and more in recent years we have come across people who, often through dabbling in occult practices, have become possessed by evil spirits. There is nothing but darkness in that experience. And only the *Holy* Spirit can drive out the unholy spirits of darkness.

But when God's Spirit takes possession, there is a marked difference. The Holy Spirit blows clean. Sometimes the change is immediately apparent; it is always ultimately clear in the fruits that spring from his presence — love, joy, peace. He burns away what defiles and pollutes. He breathes the wind of God into our lives. He brings holiness, for 'holy' is his distinctive title — over ninety times in the New Testament he is called the '*Holy*' Spirit (though seldom in the Old Testament).

So often we want power and victory in our lives, but the real question is, Do we want holiness? 'Blessed are those who hunger and thirst after *righteousness*,' Jesus said. But holiness is not a popular virtue: its standards are too high, its demands too rigorous. No wonder that the Holy Spirit, on these terms, is not very popular either. He is the very Spirit of holiness.

c. His power
The third word in the Holy Spirit's title speaks of his power: he is *Spirit*. Every picture of the Holy Spirit in the Bible is of something on the move.

He is fire: blazing and roaring in restless, endless movement. A flame is never still.

He is flowing oil: elusive, penetrating, moving. Once oil leaves its container it is almost impossible to catch it or stop it.

He is a bubbling spring: water in its most mobile

form, gushing from the ground in an endless, vital stream.

But the most common picture of the Holy Spirit in the Bible is that of a howling gale. The hymn-writer may speak of 'the gentle voice we hear, soft as the breath of even', but the fact is that the Hebrew word chosen for the Spirit of God is 'ruach', and 'ruach' is air strongly on the move, a 'rushing, mighty wind'. The wind of God exists to get God's people on the move.

The power of the wind is enormous, virtually irresistible. Twenty-four years ago I lived and worked in the Shetlands. There winds sometimes reach 120 miles an hour — strong enough to push old gravestones over or remove cottage roofs. To combat it the islanders lay their grave-stones horizontally, and use ropes and boulders to secure their roofs. It is that element, the wind, which most nearly represents the activity of God's Spirit.

As Jesus pointed out to Nicodemus, you cannot control the wind, nor even tell where it comes from and where it is going. You never know where the Holy Spirit will take you. We are born of this Spirit and baptised in this Spirit. His invisible, uncontrollable energy gives us life and then drives us on, wherever he wills.

And therein is another barrier we raise against the Holy Spirit. As human beings, we crave security, especially in our religious lives. We expect to be cocooned from change and disturbance, and look to our religion to buttress that sense of the familiar and secure.

But those who live 'in the Spirit' cannot have that kind of insurance against change. The wind blows and moves things, and we never know in which direction he will drive us next. The Holy Spirit may be a Comforter, but he is not very comfortable! All we can know for

sure is that the best place to be is the place where the
Holy Spirit takes us — wherever that may be.

2. What he does

The Holy Spirit is often called the 'executor'. That is to
say, like the person named in a will to carry out its
provisions, he sees that we get what someone else has
died to make ours. Jesus' bequest to us is his peace
(My peace I leave with you . . .). The Holy Spirit makes
the peace of Jesus ours. What the Father wills and the
Son makes possible, the Holy Spirit does.

a. Creation

The creation of the world is a perfect example of this.
The Father ordered it ('Let there be light . . .'), the Son
was involved ('Without him nothing was made . . .')
but the Spirit hatched it out ('The Spirit of God brooded
over the waters').

As we look at what God has made we see wonder,
order and beauty, and those are the hall-marks of the
creative Spirit. He is a Being of infinite variety, always
creatively active, never simply doing the same thing
over and over again but making everything new.

We need this freshness of the Holy Spirit in the
Church today. We need his creativity to do something
new, rather than endlessly repeat what was done in
our grandparents' day. It is a mark of the Holy Spirit
when the Church is creatively involved in doing a new
thing in a new way.

6. Israel

It was the Holy Spirit who brought Israel into being and
maintained its existence against all the odds. And he
usually did it by taking ordinary men and women and
making them extraordinary.

Samson is often called the strongest man in the Bible, but actually he was weak. He had no strength apart from the Holy Spirit, and when the Spirit left him his great strength left him too.

Solomon is known for his wisdom, but actually he was foolish. That is obvious from his behaviour when he was left to his own devices. Only when the Spirit was upon him did he show that wisdom for which he is justly famous.

And the same could be said for so many great figures of the Old Testament: Elijah, Abraham, Gideon, David, Moses, Amos, Jeremiah. The one thing they had in common was that they were ordinary men filled with God's extraordinary Spirit. 'The Spirit of the Lord came upon him' is the sign in the Bible that extraordinary accomplishments were about to ensue.

c. The Bible

The Holy Spirit gave us the Bible. 'Holy men of God wrote as they were moved by the Holy Spirit'. Not one of its authors knew he was writing part of the Bible at the time, yet there is a consistent unity throughout which testifies to the presence of the Holy Spirit in the whole operation. He took over the minds of the authors, so that what they wrote, God wrote. So, over a period of 1400 years, forty authors working in at least three languages produced, under his control, the unified revelation of God. That is why those who read the Bible need the Holy Spirit's aid to interpret it. After all, he is the author, and so is also the best interpreter.

d. Christ

Every part of Christ's ministry on earth was done in the power of the Holy Spirit. Jesus became man as the Son of Mary through the Holy Spirit ('conceived by the

Holy Ghost'), and every stage in his ministry was touched by his influence. At his baptism the Holy Spirit descended visibly in the form of a dove. He began his first sermon, shortly afterwards, with these words: 'The Spirit of the Lord is upon me.' His miracles were the work of the Spirit — 'If I by the Spirit of God cast out demons' — and at every phase of his life, death and resurrection, the third Person of the Trinity was involved.

e. The Church

The Holy Spirit gave us the Church. After the resurrection, Christ's followers, the embryonic Church and his sole representatives on earth, were a frightened, subdued group of men. It took the resurrection and the outpouring of the Holy Spirit at Pentecost to get them going and send them out. Subsequently every aspect of the life of the Church has been marked by the work of the Spirit — its worship, ministry, evangelism and service.

Without him a church is merely a club. It can raise money, recruit members, erect buildings, perform rituals — but without the Holy Spirit it will not be a church.

With its Head, Christ, back in heaven, and his Body, the Church, on earth, a substitute, or vicar, is needed to guide and sustain its life. The Holy Spirit is the true Vicar of Christ. Without him, we shall achieve nothing of any lasting value, however impressive our visible achievements.

Dr. Carl Bates has said, 'If God were to take the Holy Spirit out of our midst today, about ninety-five per cent of what we are doing in our churches would go on, and we would not know the difference.' I fear that may well be true, and if it is, it is simply because human beings have been trying to do 'in the flesh' what can only properly be done 'in the Spirit'. Our services, Sunday schools, choir practices, men's clubs and women's meetings have to be judged by this criterion: could they continue without the Holy Spirit? If they can, then they are products of human effort, not the divine Spirit.

The result of our neglect of him is obvious all around us. There is sameness — no creativity. There is deadness — no life. And there is sinfulness — no sanctification.

The Church cannot be full of the Holy Spirit unless its individual members are full of him. And to achieve that there must be a genuine thirst for the Spirit, together with a genuine willingness to drink of the Spirit.

The story is told of a group of sailors marooned on a life-raft off Brazil. After a few days without water they were on the verge of death, and were rescued by a passing ship in the nick of time. When they were safely on board, their rescuers asked them why they were so thirsty, to which they replied that they had no water.

'No water? You had only to reach over the side of your raft for an endless supply of water.' They had been passing through the freshwater stream that pushes right out into the Atlantic from the mighty Amazon river. The shortage was illusory. All they had needed to do was drink!

So many in the Church are like that, suffering an illusory shortage of the Holy Spirit. But he is there, all around, waiting to be invited and released. How tragic that a church can perish while its salvation surrounds it!

11: Turned On

Daddy Long Legs is a book which was enormously popular with a previous generation. It told the story of a little orphaned girl and her mysterious, anonymous benefactor. Only once had she ever seen the man who provided her with gifts and little luxuries, and then she saw only his shadow, distorted by the light so that he appeared long, thin and spidery — hence her name for him, 'Daddy Long Legs'.

Sadly, and incredibly, that is a picture of the relationship many Christians have with the Holy Spirit. They know he exists. They receive blessings and gifts from him from time to time. But he remains a mysterious, anonymous benefactor, a shadowy figure with whom they have no direct personal contact at all.

One reason for this is that so much of the Holy Spirit's work *is* done anonymously. We are aware of the results, but not of the origin. This is especially true in three areas.

In the matter of the conviction of sin, the Holy Spirit makes us inwardly aware of sin, righteousness and judgment — but we may not, and probably will not, be aware of him as a Person at the time. People have described to me a sensation they have called 'sitting on a drawing pin all through the service' — so painfully aware were they that what was being said was directed at their own sins and shortcomings. Manifestly this was not the preacher's work. As often as not the person was completely unknown to him. It was the work of the Holy Spirit, carried on through a human agent.

This is also true in the matter of the Christian's new life. The person who repents and believes in Jesus finds his life changes. His choices change. His interests change. His motivation changes.

Before he found the company of Christians embarrassing or disturbing. Now he finds it stimulating and satisfying. The Bible, which before he found boring and incomprehensible, becomes important and fascinating. All of this is the work of the Holy Spirit, but done anonymously. The believer may be quite unaware of the cause of all this change.

And it is also true in the matter of teaching — or rather, learning. The things of God are literally beyond human interpretation or comprehension. 'Who has known the mind of the Lord?' Yet the Holy Spirit can take the words of the Bible, or the words of a human preacher, and so light them up that the believer suddenly sees right through to the heart of the matter, and says 'I see . . . I see!' The Holy Spirit has been his teacher . . . anonymously.

He is the Person behind the scenes, the Person in the wings on the stage of our universe. All that happens in the world in fulfilment of God's will is his work.

But the fact that he is so self-effacing should not mean that we ignore him, or overlook the possibility and privilege of knowing him personally. I am convinced that the Christian has the tremendous privilege of knowing all three Persons of the Godhead personally and consciously. And I am equally convinced that many Christians lack that experience, and suffer through that lack.

One explanation is often given for the absence of a direct experience of the Holy Spirit in the Church. It is said that the days when such an experience was generally available have passed. That was only for the apostolic era. Today we are to know Jesus, but our experience of the Holy Spirit will necessarily be an indirect one. I believe that view is an excuse, not an explanation. Indeed, it seems to me to be almost precisely the reverse of the truth.

I believe the real explanation for the Church's neglect of an experience of the Holy Spirit lies much deeper. Indeed, I would trace it back to a man who lived before Christ, the Greek philosopher Aristotle. He said that 'the only realities are those which can be observed with the senses and deduced by reason from that observation.' His rationalism, his rejection of anything supernatural, has profoundly influenced the whole of Western thinking since his day, and it still influences it today.

Thomas Aquinas, a medieval theologian who has deeply influenced both Roman Catholic and Protestant theologians over the last 800 years, translated Aristotle's principles into theological terms. His rational approach had little room for supernatural experiences of the Holy Spirit.

The great Reformers, who rediscovered so many lost truths of Scripture — men like Luther and Calvin — failed to rediscover this one. Indeed, their approach to truth was often as 'rationalistic' as their Roman opponents! Consequently our Western culture became indoctrinated with rationalism. It had no place for visions and dreams, no room for the supernatural.

Happily the Holy Spirit has not been without his witnesses all through those ages. Various groups of Christians have maintained a living testimony to the fact that the Holy Spirit can be known and experienced personally and consciously. The Anabaptists, of the immediate post-Reformation period, knew this experi-

ence. So did the early Quakers. So did the French
Huguenots, who, according to John Wesley, spoke in
tongues. So, for that matter, did the early Methodists, as
the Holy Spirit performed signs and wonders during
that eighteenth century period of revival. And so did the
various holiness movements of the last century and the
great pentecostal movement of this century. All of these
groups witnessed to the fact that ordinary Christians
can have a direct and personal contact with the Holy
Spirit.

There are, I believe, four things concerned with the
Holy Spirit which are the privilege of every believer.
I do not believe that they should be urged on people,
nor should Christians be forced or moulded into an
experience for which they are not yet ready. However,
these *are* their privileges, and they are the birthright of
every Christian.

1. A personal introduction

The first of them we have already mentioned: the right
of each believer to enter into a conscious relationship
with each Person of the Trinity, Father, Son and Holy
Spirit. The full Christian experience involves repenting
towards God, believing in Jesus and 'receiving' Holy
Spirit. In the New Testament these three steps in
Christian initiation are clearly set out. Christians were
introduced to all three Persons, and whenever that did
not happen — and at least five times in the New Testament record people were saved but had not yet 'received
Holy Spirit' — steps were taken to put things right.

But in more recent times we have tended to run the
second and third experiences into one. We have equated
receiving the Holy Spirit with 'receiving' Jesus, but
clearly these two experiences are not identical. The New
Testament calls us to *believe* in Jesus and *receive* Holy

Spirit. The only references to 'receiving' Jesus are in John 1: 12, and Colossians 2: 6. The former clearly has an historical reference: 'He came to his own (the Jews) and his own did not receive him. But to as many (Jews) as did receive him he gave the right to become Sons of God.' The reference here, surely, is to Jesus *in the flesh*, Jesus in first century Judea. It was then literally possible to 'receive' him into your home, for example. Apostolic evangelistic preaching *never* invited people to 'receive' Jesus or 'invite him in'. Colossians 2: 6 is addressed to Christians (and the Greek word translated 'received' is a compound one which includes a sense of 'taught about' as well as 'introduced to'). Revelation 3: 20 is likewise addressed to believers already in the Church.

On every other occasion when God is spoken of as entering the life of the believer, it is in the Person of the Holy Spirit. Various verbs describe this experience: he comes upon, falls on, is poured out upon; believers are filled with, baptised in, anointed or sealed by Holy Spirit. There is a variety of experience, but it is all a direct, conscious, personal experience of the Holy Spirit.

Billy Graham has said, 'The time has come to give the Holy Spirit his rightful place. We need to learn what it means to be baptised with the Holy Spirit.'

If we do learn it, we shall find it an overwhelming experience. A Methodist minister wrote to me to say that for him being baptised in Holy Spirit was like 'taking a bath in Jesus' love'. That apparently daring expression is in fact not a bad paraphrase of the words 'baptised in the Spirit'. A more precise description of the experience has been given by American psychiatrist Morton Kelsey, who wrote that in this experience 'the individual whose ego is intact is submerged in the unconscious and emerges cleansed and restored from the dip.'

However one describes it, this personal introduction to the Holy Spirit is the privilege of everyone who believes in Jesus.

2. Spiritual ability

When we come to Christ, we come complete with our natural aptitudes and abilities and we give them to him. He may use some, and he may not use others. What is certain is that any gift of ours which he does use will first be 'anointed' by the Holy Spirit — and what a change that 'drop of oil' makes.

Without it, whatever we do brings glory to us. But when our gifts are anointed by the Holy Spirit, they bring glory to God.

However, when we have said that, we have not, as some wrongly suppose, said all there is to say about gifts and abilities. After all, not many of us are highly gifted by nature. God's family is not notably more gifted than the rest of the human race. True, most churches are run by those who bring natural gifts and aptitudes — music, administration, or manual skill — and give them to Christ. But how limited our concept of 'gifts' is if we stop there. And how impoverished the Church is, too. For another of the believer's privileges is to receive supernatural gifts from the Holy Spirit.

He is the great Giver, Himself a gift (indeed, *the* gift of God), one of his chief functions is to give gifts, presents, to God's children. For the most part, these gifts are given for the benefit of others, but this does not mean they are not gifts to us.

In Paul's first letter to the Corinthians (in chapter twelve) he lists some of these gifts. Many, if not most of them, will lie well outside the previous experience of the recipient. These are not natural gifts enhanced, but supernatural gifts freely conveyed to believers.

These gifts regularly used and developed become ministries. Teaching regularly used produces teachers. Prophecy developed and employed produces prophets. It is not the other way round. The gifts make the office, not the office the gifts.

Most of these gifts are connected with the natural gift of speech. That is especially true of tongues and prophecy.

Tongues — as it is usually called — is in many ways the gift for beginners. It gives help where at that stage it is most needed, in praise and prayer, where the novice may find himself tongue-tied and hesitant. It is not the highest gift, but neither is it, as some seem to imply, just a matter of hysterical babbling. After all, that ugly word 'tongues' simply means 'languages', and this gift is a gift of language. God gave it to the infant Church. Paul used it as much as anyone and approved of it. Perhaps its other chief value is that it is non-rational. It runs absolutely counter to the spirit of the age. It emphasises the supernatural and, for the new convert, separates mind and mouth, delivering him from a merely cerebral or 'rational' Christian experience.

Prophecy is a more advanced gift. It is not inspiring preaching, though like preaching it exists to serve and help others. Prophecy is the uttering of a message in your own language, directly inspired by the Holy Spirit. The 'prophet' is simply a messenger. He has something to pass on, exactly as it was given. And often the messenger is one who is not, and perhaps could never be, a preacher.

These gifts of speech are important. Our God is a God who speaks. Words are at the very heart of Christianity. But more than that: the mouth is so powerful an organ that it can create or destroy. James tells us in his Letter how it can be set alight by flames of hell. Yet this same faculty of speech, redeemed and anointed, can be the means of extraordinary blessing to others. You can say things from God that will minister to others — things that you could never speak in your own power.

So when *the* Gift, the Holy Spirit, is given, he gives gifts. And it is right and proper that we should 'covet' those gifts. The Bible condemns worldly coveting, but actually commands Christians to covet — earnestly desire to have — the gifts of the Holy Spirit.

3. Growing maturity

The third privilege that can be ours through the Holy Spirit is a growing maturity. This is not the result of the gifts of the Spirit, as some seem to think. The gifts of the Spirit do not necessarily make you a better or more mature Christian — look at the Church of Corinth with its squabbles and sins and unsound doctrine! The gifts are to help others, not ourselves. And it is tragically possible to have all the gifts of the Holy Spirit and remain a carnal, selfish Christian.

But the Holy Spirit does want to make us holy. He *is* concerned with our sanctification. But it is not, and cannot be, a single, sudden gift. Holiness is the product of growth in the Holy Spirit.

There are two common errors, two extremes, in this matter of Christian 'holiness'. One extreme says there is no such thing. We shall never be holy until we get to heaven, so there is not much point trying to attain it.

The other extreme says that holiness can be received in a single, once-for-all experience, after which it is virtually impossible for the believer to sin. This notion of 'perfectionism' has been preached from convention to convention, offering instant holiness through a single, dramatic experience of the Holy Spirit.

Both of these extreme views are wrong. Holiness is God's will for his people, but it is achieved, not through receiving his gifts but through walking in the Spirit. There is no short cut. As we walk in the Spirit, the fruit of the Spirit grows.

Someone once asked D. L. Moody whether he had been filled with the Spirit. 'Yes', he replied, 'but I leak.' The New Testament command is to 'go on being filled' — a process rather than a crisis. This is not instant holiness, but habitual holiness, the habit of walking in the Spirit producing the fruit of self-discipline.

The point about walking is that it is a measured means of progress. We are not called to make erratic leaps towards holiness, but a steady, step by step process leading to the goal of maturity.

The fact is that many Christians have never moved from the seventh chapter of Romans to the eighth. The seventh chapter describes a common Christian experience, in which the inside wishes to please God but the outside constantly fails. This is a kind of spiritual spastic condition in which a believer is the captive of his own bad habits, torn between what he knows he should be and what he knows he is.

But this is not meant to be the constant experience of the Christian. He is meant to go on into the experience described in chapter eight — the *normal* Christian life. Here 'the Spirit of life in Christ Jesus sets me free from the law of sin and death.' This experience is meant to be ours. It is one of the privileges of life in the Spirit, but there are no short-cuts into it.

The holiness we are called to is not an individualistic affair. It is wholeness, completeness — and we can never be whole or complete on our own. It is God's plan for the whole body, and love — mutual love — is its mark. We can have ability without love, as Paul explains in 1

Corinthians 13, but we cannot have maturity without it. It is the hall-mark of holiness.

4. Physical transformation

Archbishop William Temple once said that Christianity is the most materialistic of all world religions. The reason for that is simple: unlike all the others, Christianity is genuinely concerned with our bodies. It is not a religion which separates soul from body. From the moment of man's creation, when he *became* a living soul (not *received* a soul), the religion of the Bible is concerned with the physical as well as the spiritual.

A heckler on Tower Hill once asked Lord Soper what shape the soul is.

'Oblong,' he replied — and he was right, for that is the shape of a human body.

'Where is the soul in the body?' came the next question.

'Where the music is in the organ,' replied Lord Soper.

That is marvellously true. You could dismantle the organ, but you would never find its music. 'Soul' is the life of the body.

Jesus was physically raised from the dead, and we are told that the Spirit who raised up Jesus will also quicken *our* mortal bodies.

That 'quickening' can also be the experience of some people now in this life, for the same Spirit can give healing to sick or injured bodies.

Again, there are two extreme views of healing. Some allege that there are no miracles of healing today — that healing belonged to an earlier era of Christianity. At the other extreme are those who would claim that to sneeze is a sin — that sickness and disease have no place at all in the life of the Christian.

The first of those views limits the Holy Spirit, the

life-giver. The second denies a self-evident fact, that we are all decaying moment by moment, and that we all eventually have to die.

But even then the life-giver is not defeated. The same Holy Spirit will raise us from the dead and give us a new, spiritual body. The local cemetery, now so quiet and still, will one day be the busiest place in town, as the dead are raised 'in the twinkling of an eye'.

All of these things — the gifts, the maturity, the life, the healing — are the privileges of every believer. They are not for some super-class of Christians. But they have to be desired, and they have to be claimed . . . and many fail to claim them.

Sometimes they fear that the gifts may be demonic and will bring anxiety and evil. Others fear the danger of counterfeit spiritual gifts. Neither is a good reason for rejecting a gift of God. Indeed, the fact that demons may seek to infiltrate or counterfeit the real thing simply proves that there *is* a real thing. Nobody bothers to counterfeit half-crowns any longer.

The asking is the important thing — how we ask, and why we ask.

We ask for God's gifts with persistence, because that proves our urgent desire for them. Jesus told of a man who knocked up his neighbour in the middle of the night to borrow food to set before an unexpected guest. He knocked . . . and he went on knocking until he got a reply. That is 'how' to ask: ask, and go on asking until you receive. (Significantly, Jesus went straight on to talk about asking for Holy Spirit — Luke 11: 13).

But that story also tells us why we ask: he wanted food to set before someone else. We do not seek the gifts of the Holy Spirit for ourselves, but for others. 'I have nothing to set before him,' said the man — and neither have we, without the Holy Spirit. We want him not so that we may use him, but so that he may use us.

The order is simple. We want him first, for himself, and so that he may have more of us. And then we want him for others, so that he may bless them through us.

And what we really want, we ask for. And what we really ask for, in the name of Jesus, we receive.

12: Count Me In

Many people who will have followed all that has been said so far in this book will be approaching this chapter with reluctance. God, Christ, the Holy Spirit, forgiveness, new life — these are doctrines they value and appreciate. But for them the Church is in a different category. People outside it say they want Christ, not the Church. And people who call themselves committed Christians and spend much of their time in Christian activities are often reluctant to commit themselves to real church membership. This is a distinctly modern phenomenon, and I think there are definite causes of it.

It is partly the fault of the Church itself. Instead of the vitalised Church described in the Bible, we have seen the crystallised Church and then the fossilised Church. We can see this in a country like Wales, where early this century there was an amazing spiritual revival. Today, most of the signs of that revival are its fossil remains — huge, empty, often derelict chapels in almost every village. About the only obvious surviving influence of that revival is its music. A spiritual movement can die out in a welter of buildings, fine language, or singing. Indeed, the Church today demonstrates its lack of vitality by its preoccupation with such things. We use Gothic architecture, Roman costumes, Elizabethan language and Victorian music! No wonder people feel we are out of touch with reality. No wonder the inspiration has become trapped in the institution.

A magazine article recently asked, 'Where has the Jesus movement gone?' It is an interesting question. The 'Jesus Movement' of the late sixties and early seventies seemed to be just that spontaneous, unplanned, exuberant outburst of Christianity that the world needed. But in its early days, it was very suspicious of the Church — afraid, doubtless, that it would institutionalise and fossilise this infant movement. In fact, the answer to the question posed by the article is a very simple one: the best part of the Jesus movement has gone into the Church. At last, it has found its true place, to the benefit of both bodies.

But in general, enthusiasm and the Church remain strangers to each other, and this is not only because the Church has failed. It is also due to the spirit of the age. Certain things are very unpopular today, like discipline, authority, commitment and involvement. We live in an age in which people want to keep themselves to themselves. They want to be free from other people, free to do 'their own thing'. In these circumstances, it is not surprising that fewer and fewer people wish to commit themselves to membership of a church.

So, why not call it quits? Why not stop the struggle to 'keep the Church going', accept defeat, and settle for a personal belief in and witness for Jesus, without membership of anything, and meetings with other believers only as and when we feel like them? Who could possibly object to that?

The short answer is, Jesus! He would not approve. That can be said quite emphatically. After all, the Church was his idea, his dream, his ambition. He has not disowned it — he bled for it, he bought it with his own blood.

The importance of the Church to Jesus can be expressed by two facts — something he did, and something he said.

When he returned to heaven from the earth, Jesus left behind him eleven hand-picked men. That number was not accidental, nor was the selection of the twelve original apostles simply a symbolical replacement for the twelve tribes of Israel. The fact is that a synagogue — a Jewish 'Church' — could only be formed when ten or more adult males came together. Jesus left behind him such a 'quorum' ... with one to spare. His witnesses were enough to form a church, according to Jewish custom.

Something he said also supports this idea. For the first two and a half years of his ministry on earth he never used the word 'church'. Then just before the Transfiguration, he asked his disciples the question he had saved for that moment: who do you say that I am? And Simon Peter became at that moment the first member of the Church. 'You are the Christ, the Son of God,' he said. And Jesus commented, 'Upon this rock — you confessing me — I will build my Church.' Jesus intended to have a Church, and he intended every Christian, everyone who shared in Peter's confession of him, to be a member of it.

The crunch question, however, is not whether Christ intended to create a Church — he obviously did; but *what kind of Church did he intend?* For us, the word 'church' evokes all sorts of images: buildings, denominations, clergy, Sunday schools, choirs and organs. But these powerful images may distort our attempts to discover what Jesus intended. For, good or bad, they are no part of the Church he founded. They all came much later. Three questions can, in fact, get us back to the heart of the matter.

1. Who should belong to the Church?

This is the first fundamental question, and in a country like Britain, where Christianity has been the dominant religion for centuries, it is extremely difficult to answer — where should we draw the line between the Church and the world? In Britain over eighty per cent of the population have been christened; about forty per cent have been confirmed, or received into membership of a church; ten per cent go to Church at Christmas and Easter; three per cent attend Church regularly — and how many really have a living relationship with Jesus? Perhaps only one or two per cent! Who knows which of those statistics represents the number of God's people, the Church?

What we do know is that it does have limits. Christ drew sharp lines around his Church, using various metaphors for the distinction he was making: sheep and goats, wheat and tares, wise and foolish virgins. Perhaps three of the New Testament's pictures of the Church help to clarify the issue.

The family of God is one such picture. It has been truly said that there are sons and daughters in God's family, but no grandsons. There is no way into a family except by birth or adoption: you cannot worm or sneak or bribe your way in. You cannot be born a Christian. Only Jesus was 'the begotten' Son of God. But we can be adopted into the family as sons and that is what we understand by being 'born again'.

Then there is the picture of *the flock of Christ* — the Shepherd and his sheep. This speaks of the personal relationship of dependence on him which unites all the members of the Church. 'I know my sheep,' he said, 'I call them by name.'

I remember watching two shepherds in Israel trying to separate their flocks which had become mingled. There were probably 200 sheep altogether and it looked an impossible task. But they set about it methodically. They picked up lambs, looked at them, recognised their own and sorted them out. The sheep were simply called by name. It was a striking illustration of the words of Jesus, and a striking illustration of the flock of Jesus. The sheep know him, and he knows them personally. They have heard the voice of Jesus and responded to it.

Then, the Church is *the fellowship of the Spirit*. This is really the out-working of Paul's clear statement in Romans 8: 'If any man have not the Spirit of Christ, he is none of his.' Only those who have the Spirit can be counted as in the fellowship.

So the Church consists of those who are related to God as his sons, to Jesus as his sheep, and to the Holy Spirit as his friends. It is that kind of relationship, a relationship made possible by the Cross, which makes the members of the true Church. They are related to God, through repentance and faith. They are truly converted, truly born again. They, and only they, make up the Church.

2. What should the Church be doing?

I remember looking from the top deck of a bus in a provincial city at the church notice boards on a main street. They gave a fascinating glimpse into what these churches saw as their main approach to outsiders. 'Grand Bazaar', said one. 'Hula Hoop Demonstration', said another. 'Special People's Services' said a third, 'Hearty singing. No sermon!'

The average church programme can be overwhelming. It is certainly not hard to have an active church. But the real question is, activity for what purpose? What are the Church's objectives? Do these activities help to achieve them?

I would suggest there are three objectives, and any church activity which does not further them should be dropped.

The first is *worship* — doing something that gives God first place. It is the only really selfless activity: 'to the praise of *his* glory'. But this activity, which is not natural to us, needs to be learned. Our worship may be liturgical or free — its form is comparatively unimportant. What is absolutely fundamental is that God should receive what he looks for, our love and our praise.

The second is *evangelism*, which is the Church representing God's message to the world. He has called us to love our neighbours, as he loved the world and gave his Son for it. But truly to love is to evangelise. How can we love a person and stand idly by while they drift into hell? Our love for our neighbour can and should be expressed in physical help, but it can and should also be expressed in spiritual help.

We have to learn evangelism: not so much how to do it, but that it should be done.

Thirdly, we should have as an objective our *fellowship* with one another. The last command of Jesus before his crucifixion was that his disciples should love each other. That is the way in which we should support our fellow-Christians. In time together, in prayer together, in acts of love and concern, we build each other up in the body of Christ. And that, too, must be learned. It will not just 'happen'.

We need to look at every activity in which our churches engage, and ask ourselves whether each is helping forward one of these objectives. If it is not helping us to praise the Lord, serve our neighbour, or build up the body of Christ, then there is no reason to waste our time and effort on it. If it is serving God (in worship), or the world (in evangelism) or the Church (in fellowship), then it is truly an activity of the body of Christ.

3. How should the Church be organised?

Many people today would say that the Church should not be organised, but free and spontaneous. They like to say that it is an organism, not an organisation.

But God is a God of order. All through the Bible we see him organising the processes of creation and redemption, and always with marvellous attention to detail. It is hardly likely that he would create a disorganised Church.

And, of course, he has not. If we examine the New Testament, we find guide-lines for the organisation of the Church. Most of the really fundamental questions are answered.

It is quite clear, for instance, that the organisation and control of the Church is not in the hands of any one man at any level. It is not the 'Reverend So-and so's church'. Leadership in the New Testament is always plural: apostles, elders, deacons. Each local church was to have several elders, not just one.

And it was to be a *local* church, neither an international nor a national set-up with a hierarchy. The Church is made up of churches — local churches, with the Christians of a given locality under local leadership.

The New Testament Church was not democratic. It did not know our enthusiasm for votes about this and that. There was a properly appointed leadership. They were not dictators, but trusted leaders; and they did not need to depend on a popular vote, though they were 'recognised' as the ascended Lord's gift.

One other factor shines through the New Testament's picture of the Church. Every Christian, without exception, was a full member of a local church.

4. What are the marks of a true church?

But what is a true church? And when is a 'church' not a church? For there can be no doubt that history is full of counterfeits and imitations of the real thing.

Let's be quite clear that a 'true' church will *not* be perfect. We should not expect to find a perfect church on earth. And, as has been truly said, if we do find a perfect church we should not join it, because then it would be imperfect!

We should expect to find, first of all, *faith*. The Church is a building made of living stones laid on a solid foundation, and that foundation is the confession of faith that Peter made before the Transfiguration. Peter's successors share Peter's faith: 'You are the Christ, the Son of the living God.' On the cornerstone of Christ, on the foundation of faith, the Church is built. Without that faith there simply is no Church.

Then, the Church is the bride of Christ — a daring metaphor used of God's people in the Old and the New Testament. Like a husband and wife, Christ and his Church are joined together in a perfect unity. This imagery speaks of *hope*: we look on to the great wedding feast of heaven which is portrayed in Revelation. We eagerly await the return of the bridegroom.

And, thirdly, the Church is a body, and this speaks of its inner life of *love*. Again the metaphor is a daring one. Each member is literally a limb or an organ of the body — like a hand, a leg, or a lung, we are part of a living organism. And what blood is to the human body, love is to the Church. It is nourished and fed by it.

It is worth emphasising that each of these marks points to Jesus Christ. He is the cornerstone of the building, the bridegroom, the head of the body. And that is the true mark of the true Church: it is totally Christ-centred, in faith, hope and love.

5. What is its future?

Some people believe that the Church has no future, that it is finished. But the facts contradict them.

Never in its history has the Church been growing as fast as it is today — more than 25,000 new members every day. It is completely and gloriously alive, with all the marks of life, with a wonderful past and an exciting future.

But what will that future hold?

The Church will certainly be *persecuted*. That was prophesied by Jesus, and how it is being fulfilled today! I believe that as the end draws nearer so that persecution will grow more intense.

Then, the future will see the Church *completed*. When Christ comes, not one member will be missing. And the great family of Christ will include people of all races, tribes and languages, of every colour and culture. God loves a mixed family.

The Church is also destined to be resurrected and *raptured*. Its members, raised from the dead, will be caught up at his coming to meet Jesus in the clouds, as Paul describes in 1 Thessalonians 4. Of course, the Church today *includes* the dead, all those believers who have lived before us. My mother and my sister, who are both dead, are still part of the Church. The gates of death shut them off temporarily from me, but not from Jesus. The Church militant (on earth) and the Church triumphant (in heaven) are one Church, not two. When Christ comes those who are alive at that time will be re-united with those who are dead.

The Church will then be *crowned*, reigning with Christ. The bride will meet her bridegroom.

I also believe that the Church will be *united*, not only with God but with his people of the former Covenant, Israel of old. 'There will be one flock and one shepherd.'

Finally, the Church will be *glorified*, raised above the angels, set in the 'new heaven and earth'. Christ has promised himself a 'glorious' Church, and finally it will share his glory when all earthly glory has faded away. It is safe to say that no other society on earth has a future like that.

So, the question is, Do I belong to this Church? For this is the 'one, holy, catholic and apostolic' Church that the creeds speak about.

One, because it has one Head, one faith, and one Spirit.

Holy, because it is different from the rest of the world, marked off, God's special people. One day every member will be perfect.

Catholic in the true meaning of the word, because it is world-wide, having no barriers of class, colour or culture, all-embracing.

And it is apostolic because it is based on the beliefs and behaviour of the apostles. It shares their faith. It is the Church of their Book, the New Testament.

This — and no other — is the Church of the Lord Jesus, which he obtained 'with his own blood'.

13: A Few Facts About the Future

There are two strangely contradictory modern attitudes towards the future. Some people say we must think more about it; others, that we should think less.

The first group are the 'futurologists', the experts who have studied what the future holds for this planet, and believe that the time has come for everybody to accept that, unless we plan for the future, there simply will not be one.

After all, they say, we live in a world of swiftly accelerating change. Many people are suffering from what Alvin Tofler labelled 'future shock', a massive adaptational breakdown. Far from being exempt from this, church members are among the prime sufferers. They find the pace of change in the Church, too, unacceptable. In every walk of life the effects of change are felt. Knowledge doubles every ten years. Discovery treads on the heels of discovery. We have broken irretrievably with the past, and are racing headlong into the future.

So, they say, we must study it. All over the world 'think tanks' are at work grappling with the enormous problems facing our planet if it is to survive. Our only hope, according to the futurologists, is to try to keep one move ahead.

But the other group — very vocal a few years ago — would reject this entirely. As the future is in such doubt, they would argue, we may as well live life to the full now, and let the future take care of itself. These are the pessimists; the people who believe that doomsday is around the corner (one 'think-tank' puts it about twenty-five years away) and there is nothing we can do about it. In these circumstances, we might as well turn our backs on the future and concentrate on the present — or even the past. So existentialism (living for the present) and nostalgia (living for the past) are both in vogue.

Whether we think we can foresee our planet's future, or whether we believe it does not have one, the important thing for the Christian to realise is that the world is not out of control, nor is it under man's control. God is in control of events, as he has always been. History, as someone has said, is 'his story'. He determines the direction and speed of world events and one day he will bring human history to an end.

So, if we are tempted to feel that things have got out of hand, or if the pace of change causes us anxiety, we need to be reminded that God not only knows what lies ahead, but has told us. Over a quarter of the Bible is predictive, and over eighty per cent of those predictions have already come true. Indeed, only about a dozen predictions remain to be fulfilled before this age ends, and the period beyond those events is ushered in. God knows the future, God plans the future ... and God *tells* the future, so that we may live the present correctly by relating ourselves to what is going to happen. God wants us to know what lies ahead, because it affects how we behave now.

As we turn to consider what God has revealed about the future, we shall find that over one or two details Bible-believing Christians hold differing opinions. But in the main, those who believe that the Bible reveals

God's truth to man agree about the general outline of
what lies ahead of us.

1. The immediate future

The immediate future is concerned with what the Bible
calls 'this present evil age'. Its picture of the world in
the final days is depressingly familiar, and covers every
aspect of life today — social, political, ecclesiastical,
natural and even spiritual.

In the *social* sphere, the 'last days' will see an emphasis
on pleasure for its own sake. Alongside this there will
be a repudiation of authority and a growth in lawless-
ness. Violence will flourish. So will immorality of every
kind. Family life will break up and there will be conflict
between social groups — capital and labour, parents
and children. The result of all this will be wide-spread,
almost universal fear. All of this is quite specifically
predicted in the words of Jesus himself.

In the *political* realm, there will be a decline of de-
mocracy and an increase in dictatorships, as frightened
people, perplexed by 'wars and rumours of wars', turn
to the 'strong men' to solve the problems of the nations
by force. Great efforts for peace and security will fail,
increasing the 'distress of nations with perplexity', as
Jesus foretold.

In all this turmoil, I believe that Israel has a vital role.
The Jewish return to Palestine and the re-establishment
of Israel seem to me events of enormous significance,
though that would need a whole book in itself.*

In the *ecclesiastical* area, the 'last days' will be
marked by compromise and weakness. In many cases,
ministers will become deceivers, false prophets, even
setting themselves up as Messiahs. The cults will

*For those interested, one of the best is: *The Rebirth of the
State of Israel: is it of God or of men?* by Arthur W. Kac, M.D.

multiply. Fables and fancies will lead men astray.

Church members will fare no better. Love of God will wax cold, there will be indifference and ignorance, and many will fall away. The result of all this will be a blurring of the line between the Church and the world.

In the *natural* realm, disasters like earthquakes, floods and pestilence will testify to the delicate relationship between man and the physical world he inhabits. There seems to be a kind of psychosomatic connection between man and nature. When man is disordered, nature is disordered, too. Ultimately, the sun, moon and stars will also be affected.

Finally, in the *spiritual* sphere, world-wide evangelism will mark the 'last days'. The Gospel of Christ will be taken to every nation, tribe and tongue — and already it has been taken to every country. Yet this increasing evangelism — and there is more evangelism being undertaken now than at any time in the Church's history — will not win the majority to Christ. 'When the Son of Man comes, shall he find faith on the earth?' Ridicule, opposition, scoffing and outright persecution will be its main result . . . as Christ foretold.

All of these events will reach their climax in the emergence of a new world ruler and what the Bible calls the 'big trouble' — the 'Great Tribulation'. Throughout the Bible — in Daniel, Matthew, 2 Thessalonians and Revelation — this is predicted.

A confederacy of ten kingdoms in the Middle East will become a new super-power, with three rulers replaced by one dominant figure, known to the Bible as 'Antichrist' (that simply means 'instead of Christ' rather than 'against Christ') usurping his place. Under this man, the state and its ruler will take the place of God. And this godless rule will lead to the final cataclysm of the Great Tribulation.

All Christians agree that the Jews will go through the tribulation. But there is a division of opinion as to whether Christians will.

The 'classical' view (the one held for many centuries) is that they will. Revelation refers to the saints who have come '*out of* great tribulation', so they must have been in it! Believers should be prepared to face this short (a few years), sharp and painful experience.

Early in the nineteenth century another view emerged. Men like Irving, Bullinger, J. N. Darby and Scofield taught that the Church would be 'raptured' — snatched away — *before* the Tribulation.

For myself, I hold to the 'classical' 'post-tribulational' view, and I would rather make the mistake of preparing the people of God for suffering even if they will escape it, than commit the more serious error of leading them into a false security! But the important thing is to stress that the next great event in world history is that Jesus is coming again.

2. Beginnings of the age to come

Antichrist is in fact to be the world's second-last leader. Christ will be the last one. During the final world war, directed at Israel, and at its height, Christ will return to his land. About this event there is no disagreement among Bible-lovers. In fact, it is referred to over three hundred times. His return will be physical and visible, and he will come this time as king — and his kingdom will come with him.

However, there is a second difference of opinion among Christians here. Where and when will Christ set up his kingdom, on earth or in heaven? Will his thousand-year reign — the 'millennium' — follow or precede his return?

Three views have appeared:

The *pre-millennial* belief is that the millennium will take place after Christ's return. This seems to me the plainest interpretation, and the plainest is usually the right one. The world will see what it could have been if it had not rejected Christ's rule.

The *post-millennial* view is that the Church will bring in the kingdom of Christ by 'christianising' the whole world, before he returns. It is an idea implicit in many Victorian missionary hymns — 'the earth shall be filled with the glory of God'.

The third view, called *a-millennial*, has been more widely held in recent years. In effect it makes the millennium a spiritual experience rather than an actual event. It is the reign of Christ in our hearts, and the current reign of Christ in heaven, of which this vision of a thousand perfect years is simply a picture.

Again, I hold to the original, pre-millennial position of the early church. I am thrilled to think of this coming demonstration *on earth* of the power of Christ. 'Thy kingdom come, thy will be done on earth as it is in heaven.'

3. The ultimate destiny

The second coming of Christ ends human history. It can be rather futile to argue about details of events and their order. What is important is to understand what will follow the return of Christ.

One thing that will certainly follow is the *resurrection of the body*. Death divides the body and soul, but they are to be reunited. Our mortal spirits will put on immortal bodies, just like Christ's own resurrection body.

Whether this resurrection is good or bad news will depend on our destiny. All are raised: the good and the bad. And each will show in his immortal body what his nature really has been: good, or bad.

This leads to the whole idea of *judgment*. There will be a day of settlement, when secret sins will be revealed and every thought, word and deed will appear as evidence. On that day there will only be two groups: the sinners, who have rejected the light they had and will now receive punishment for sins; and the saints, the believers, whose judgment is solely one of reward for service. But the judge is the same in both cases, Jesus Christ.

Then — however much we may rebel at the thought — there is the *punishment of the wicked*. Like everyone else, I can raise many objections to the whole idea of God's punishment of his creatures: moral, philosophical, psychological and theological objections. But all fall before the words of Christ. Only once in the whole of the Bible is the word 'hell' found on any other lips than his. He — the Friend of sinners, the Saviour of the world, the messenger of love — is the one who tells us of hell, a place where body and soul are in torment. It has been prepared for the devil and his angels, and they will be joined by godless men. Hell, quite simply, is to be without him who is goodness, light and love; and is therefore all that is bad, dark and hateful.

But *blessedness* — heaven — is to be with him, and that is the destiny of the saints. Heaven is where Christ is. Indeed, it is where God himself is, filling it all. In heaven there is no need for a temple, a holy place. It is all holy.

I believe it is a place — a city, if you like — of such splendour that the greatest splendours of the earth pall before it. And in that splendid city a place is prepared for each believer, a personal share in the glory of God.

And finally there will be the *re-creation of the universe*. This one will be dissolved by its own energy. And from the fire God will forge a new heaven and a new earth in a new universe.

All of these events, from the emergence of anti-Christ to the new creation, will surely come to pass. Some of us may not personally experience the first set of events — those leading up to the coming of Christ. But every single one of us will experience the rest. Resurrection and judgment will come to all. They are part of our future, come what may.

So the final question is this: what is our response to it all? 'Since all these things are thus to be dissolved, what sort of persons ought you to be . . . ?' (2 Peter 3: 11).

14: The Book Behind This One

I have saved for this last chapter the key-stone of the whole book. All along I have invited the reader to share my assumption that what the Bible teaches is what Christians believe, and that it is true.

Now that is, in itself, a massive claim, and obviously one cannot complete a book which purports to set out the heart of Christian truth without examining the primary source of that truth. And the primary source, beyond any doubt, is the Bible, which Christians call the 'Word of God'. If the Bible is untrue, unreliable or untrustworthy, then all the previous chapters of this book are built on sand, and you might as well throw them away.

When our present Queen was crowned in Westminster Abbey, there came a moment which was for me the most memorable incident in the whole service. The Moderator of the General Assembly of the Church of Scotland handed her a Bible, with these words: 'Here is the most valuable thing this world affords.' What an incredible claim for any book — more valuable than the gold deposits of South Africa or the technology of the United States, or the plays of Shakespeare or the paintings of Michelangelo. The Moderator then added: 'This is the royal law.' This book, in other words, is the law for monarchs. The Queen and her

Parliament make the laws of Britain, but God makes laws for her!

With claims of that dimension made for it, it is not surprising that Christianity has been called the 'religion of a Book'. But more staggering still are the claims the Bible makes for itself, as we shall now see.

1. The claims the Bible makes for itself

(a) *Its inspiration*

The Bible claims to be a supernatural book. 'All Scripture is inspired by God', wrote Paul — but the actual verb he used means 'expired' . . . 'breathed-out,' as all words are. The Bible is God-breathed. It came from his mouth, it is his direct revelation to mankind. What we could never find out for ourselves, God has made plain to us in this Book.

God inspired the writings (2 Timothy 3: 16) and the writers (2 Peter 1: 10). The ideas in the Bible are not the opinions or even beliefs of human minds. They are the ideas of God expressed through the minds and words of men. This does not mean that the writers were mere typewriters, mechanically reproducing words which God put in their minds, but rather that the writers were so 'moved' by the Holy Spirit, so much under his control, that he could use their human personalities and characteristics to express his revelation without their human limitations distorting or confusing it. The Bible is the Word of God in the words of men. It says exactly what he wants to say.

Incidentally, when we say the Bible is 'inspired' we do not just mean that it is 'inspiring', though much of it is. Inspiration is what God has done to the Book, not what the Book has done to me.

(b) *Its integrity*

If the Bible is to be the Word of God it must be absolutely reliable and trustworthy. It cannot contain error, contradiction or discrepancy, because God is a God of *truth*. This, for many people, is the biggest problem about the Bible, bceause it does appear to contain some contradictions. The Gospel accounts of the resurrection of Jesus are an example of this.

There was a time when I thought that there were discrepancies and contradictions of this kind in the Bible. What I now see that I was doing was trying to measure the infinite wisdom of God with a tiny human brain.

In fact, as I have gone further into the Scriptures and studied them more closely, I have found that many apparent discrepancies have vanished. As any detective will confirm, when many witnesses tell the truth about an event, their accounts will have *apparent* discrepancies and contradictions. Beware of the perfect alibi! But closer examination will show that the 'discrepancies' actually fit into the pattern of the truth.

I discovered, for instance, that most if not all of the apparent discrepancies in the Gospel accounts of the resurrection (how could it be 'after three days and nights' or even 'on the third day' if he died on Friday afternoon and rose *before dawn* on Sunday?) disappeared when one discovered that the Romans counted a day from midnight to midnight, and the Jews from six p.m. to six p.m.; and that Jesus died not on Friday (as we have all assumed), but on a Wednesday afternoon! Then everything fitted perfectly!

Of course, some problems still remain — some of them problems of translation. But I am content to believe God and to wait until the *whole* truth becomes plain.

(c) Its injunctions

The Bible also claims *authority*. It is not a book of
opinions, even divine ones. If the Bible is the Word of
God it is the absolute and final authority and my response to it is to put myself under it. The Church is
'under' it. Reason is 'under' it. The only question I need
raise is, 'What do the words mean?'

The Bible has been caricatured as the 'paper Pope of
Protestantism'. With the reservation that we do not
worship the actual book (which would be bibliolatry),
nor regard it as the 'vicar of Christ', I would accept the
title for the Bible.

It is the infallible source of truth. As St. Augustine
wrote, 'To the canonical Scriptures alone I owe agree-
ment without dissent.' And Luther said, 'My conscience
is captive to the Word of God.'

(d) Its instruction

The Bible is also a sufficient source of instruction. It
was on this that the Reformation turned: Scripture
is all we need. Commentaries, Bible notes and even
preachers are only helpful if they drive us back to
the Bible itself. Here is enough for all our needs, both
as to what we should believe and how we should
behave.

(e) Its interpretation

The Bible is its own interpreter. The answer to the
common question, 'How are we to interpret or understand the meaning of Scripture?' is that it is self-
explanatory. The key to Scripture is Scripture itself.
Very often we can use a simple passage to illuminate
and open up a difficult one. Certainly we should com-
pare Scripture with Scripture, the Old Testament with
the New. What is certain is that the Bible cannot contra-

dict itself — but we need to read *all* of it in order to understand *any* of it fully.

(*f*) *Its interest*

It is often said that the Bible is boring, and it is not a sufficient answer to say, 'On the contrary, it is fascinating.' Truth to tell, much of it *is* boring and dull unless you know what you are looking for. It only becomes fascinating when we become spiritually alive, because it is a spiritual book that can be appreciated only at the spiritual level. But when we approach it correctly — that is, with the right motivation and guided by the Spirit — it *is* fascinating. John Wesley recalled a time in his life when he wanted to know 'one thing, how to get to heaven'. His cry was simple: 'Give me that Book!' Like the parables of Jesus, the whole of Scripture is for those with eyes and ears open spiritually. 'He who has ears to hear, let him hear.'

(*g*) *Its intention*

The Bible is clear about its own intention, which is to answer that desire of John Wesley's. It is a book about getting to heaven. God brought it into being not to entertain (and a great deal of it is very far from entertaining!), nor to educate in history or science, nor to give the human race a handbook of ethics — though there is good history, good science and good ethics in it. The Scriptures are given to make us 'wise unto *salvation*'. That is their intention. They are to provide that knowledge of God and Christ which brings salvation; and they are to feed the new-born believer.

2. Can these claims be substantiated?

Now everyone would agree that the elements listed above are what the Bible claims for itself. But normally we do not accept a self-evaluation. Are there any convincing reasons for believing these to be valid claims? I should like to suggest seven.

(a) Its survival

The Bible has been more fiercely attacked and over a longer period than any book in history. It has suffered physical attacks — banning and burning. It has suffered intellectual attacks of scorn and derision. Yet it still not only survives, but flourishes. One of its fiercest denunciators was the French writer Voltaire, who predicted that within a hundred years of his death the Bible would be found only in museums. The house where Voltaire lived in Paris became a Bible Society's headquarters!

The Bible faces no new criticisms. Indeed, alleged 'discrepancies' produced at regular intervals as though they were new discoveries were in fact raised in the second century by writers like Celsus, Porphyry, Lucius and Diocletian. It has weathered all such storms many times, and will continue to do so.

For only one year in modern history has the Bible not been the best-seller in Britain. The exception was 1962, when D. H. Lawrence's *Lady Chatterley's Lover* — the subject of a notorious court case — swept to the top. Some people gloomily predicted that the Bible could no longer be called the best-selling book. They need not have worried. In 1963 it was back at number one, and has stayed there ever since.

It has been translated into over two thousand languages, and is more widely read today than ever in its stormy history. 'Heaven and earth will pass away,' said Jesus, 'but my words will not pass away.'

(b) Its unity

The Bible is really sixty-six books by some forty

different authors writing over a period of about 1,500 years in three languages, Hebrew, Aramaic and Greek. There was no human editor and no organising committee. Yet the book has a total unity.

From Genesis to Revelation the Bible has one theme: our salvation in Christ. And it has one ultimate author, the Holy Spirit. That is how it comes about that every part contributes to the whole. Poetry, epic, prose, letters, proverbs — every literary form — combine to pursue the one great theme. It is a living Book with a living Author.

(c) *Its inexhaustibility*

A little girl asked an old lady why she spent so much time reading her Bible.

'I'm studying for my finals,' was the reply.

This is a book that repays study, and even at the end of a life-time there is still more to find. I am perpetually amazed how I can return to a passage I know well and read it as though for the first time, seeing new truths and new perspectives I had previously missed. That is a mark of the depth of the divine inspiration of the Bible. You can never say 'I know this Book.' The greatest intellects have never plumbed its depths, simply because man can only exhaust what man has produced.

(d) *Its relevance*

Have you ever sat in a hotel bedroom and read the fly-leaf of a Gideon Bible? 'Are you anxious?' it asks — and refers the anxious reader to some relevant passages. 'Are you lonely? Frightened? Distressed?' And, of course, the files of the Gideons are full of stories of people who have looked up the verses and felt that God was speaking directly to them.

That is another hallmark of the Bible: its relevance.

It is timeless, but it is also timely. All over the world, to people of all races and cultures, to young and old, to people in their prime, to the dying, the Bible speaks in a way no other book can do. What an influence it has been down the centuries on men and women of utterly contrasting back-grounds!

(e) *Its predictions*
In the previous chapter we saw how accurately the Bible has predicted the future.

The fairest test of a prophecy is its fulfilment. By that test the Bible stands alone. Nearly 600 of the events predicted in scripture have already come true!

For example, many details of the birth, life, death and resurrection of Jesus were foretold in the Old Testament. Every single one came true. Only one Person in the universe knows the future like this: God. It seems no exaggeration, then, to call the Bible God's Word.

(f) *Jesus' attitude*
Jesus undoubtedly believed the Bible to be the Word of God. 'It is written,' was constantly on his lips — he used the Old Testament to defeat Satan in the wilderness. He specifically endorsed every part of the Old Testament. He called the Pentateuch — the books of the Law — the 'Word of God'. Not one jot (the smallest letter) nor tittle (a point like our dots and crossed t's) was to pass away. He said of the Psalms, 'The Scripture cannot be broken,' and included the prophets in his list of the Scriptures, too.

The New Testament, of course, was not written until some time after the life-time of Jesus, but he promised its writers a special gift of the Holy Spirit to bring to remembrance all that he had told them and to reveal further things for which they were not ready during his earthly life (John 14: 26 and 16: 12). Peter refers to Paul's writings as 'scripture' (2 Peter 3: 15, 16) and Paul himself claimed to write at the express command of the Lord: 'We impart this in words not taught by human wisdom but taught by the Spirit.'

(g) The Holy Spirit's 'proof'

In some ways the most convincing of all the evidence for the claims of the Bible, cannot be shared with those who are sceptical about them.

This is the 'inner testimony' — the Holy Spirit's witness in our hearts to his authorship of the Bible. It is the clinching evidence for the Christian, but it cannot be discovered by the intellect and sometimes the cleverest people miss it entirely.

It is this testimony which speaks to faith. 'My sheep hear my voice,' said Jesus, and we can hear his voice through the words of Scripture. This confirms that it is a *living* word, speaking in my heart to my deepest needs. The nearer you get to someone, the more you believe their words; and the nearer we get to God, the more confidence we will have in his Word.

One day we shall throw away our Bibles, because we shall not need them any more. I still have my old school-books stacked away somewhere in a box in the house, but I do not know why I have kept them. They fulfilled their purpose long ago, and now they are only of nostalgic value.

Equally, even the Bible will eventually be overtaken by history. When Christ returns and the Church is complete, all its truth will have been told, all its prophecies fulfilled. We simply shall not need it any longer, for God's presence will make his words our immediate experience.

But until then we need the Bible . . . and *how* we need

it! We need the living voice of a living God coming to us through its pages, telling truth.

And this Book *is* truth. Not just inspiring, but inspired, a God-breathed revelation. When all is said and done, that is the heart of the matter: the words of the Bible are the words of God, and to those words we must listen. Truth to hear gives us truth to tell.

Teach Me The Truth

Teach me the truth, Lord, though it put to flight
 My cherished dreams and fondest fancy's play;
Give me to know the darkness from the light,
 The night from day.

Teach me the truth, Lord, though my heart may break
 In casting out the falsehood for the true;
Help me to take my shattered life and make
 Its actions new.

Teach me the truth, Lord, though my feet may fear
 The rocky path that opens out to me;
Rough it may be, but let the way be clear
 That leads to Thee.

Teach me the truth, Lord. When false creeds decay,
 When man-made dogmas vanish with the night,
Then, Lord, on Thee my darkened soul shall stay,
 Thou living Light.

FRANCES LOCKWOOD GREEN
Quoted in *Has Christ's Return Two Stages?* by
Norman F. Douty, published by Pageant Press Inc.
New York.